How Then Should We Eat The Lord's Supper

By

Robert A. French

Copyright © 2013 by Robert A. French

How Then Should We Eat the Lord's Supper
by Robert A. French

Printed in the United States of America
ISBN 9781626979482

All rights reserved solely by the author. The author guarantees all contents are original and do not infringe upon the legal rights of any other person or work. No part of this book may be reproduced in any form without the permission of the author. The views expressed in this book are not necessarily those of the publisher.
Unless otherwise indicated, Bible quotations are taken from New English Translation (NET). Copyright © 1996-2006 by Biblical Studies Press, L.L.C. http://netbible.com. Scripture quoted by permission. All rights reserved. The names: the NET bible®, new english translation copyright (c) 1996 by biblical studies press, l.L.C. Net bible® is a registered trademark the net bible® logo, service mark copyright (c) 1997 by biblical studies press, l.L.C. All rights reserved satellite imagery copyright (c) røhr productions ltd. And centre national d'études spatiales photographs copyright (c) røhr productions ltd. Scripture taken from the Holy Bible, New International Version. Copyright 1973, 1978, 1984 International Bible Society. Used by permission of Zondervan Bible Publishers.

www.xulonpress.com

TABLE OF CONTENTS

1. Rituals, Ceremonies, & Symbolism 9
2. Old Covenant or New 17
3. What Does It Matter 25
4. The Passover 31
5. Sacrament of Communion 35
6. An Examination of John Chapter Six 41
7. Take, Eat, This Is My Body 57
8. John 6:63 85

Short Bio of the Author

Robert (Bob) French has been in the ministry for over fifty years and during that time he has been an evangelist, a pastor, and missionary and has ministered in many countries and islands of the sea. He is now pastor of Balance Life Christian Fellowship in the city of St. Charles Missouri near St. Louis. Through the years Bro. French has conducted tent and auditorium meetings as well as speaking in hundreds of churches. He has pioneered in several places including the island of Puerto Rico where he and his wife spent three years in the San Juan area. Bro. French has spent a great deal of time working in Mexico and along with his oldest son Brian was privileged to spend a good deal of time in the mountains of Chiapas Mexico ministering to the indigenous Indians of the area where they saw God move in miraculous ways. He spends most of his time these days ministering to his local congregation and writing, but still takes occasional speaking engagements in other areas as he is able to do so.

Acknowledgements

I want to especially thank my wife Sandy, and other members of my family for their support and encouragement while writing this book.

I also want to thank my brother in Christ and long time friend Robert Keranen for his thoughts and insights on this subject, which were very helpful to me in several areas.

INTRODUCTION

From the birth, death and resurrection of Jesus men have attempted to follow him by building narrow structures around doctrines that may or may not reflect the truth of the Scripture they suppose to base it on. Many Christian religions, when teaching about their foundational doctrine on which they base their faith, refer the seeker to the tradition of their particular church rather than the biblical basis. Traditions appear in many ways in formal religion, but the most obvious is in ceremonial and sacramental worship. In the pages that follow, I will attempt to show the importance and the absolute necessity of getting past the traditions of men. It is not my intention here to attack religions, but rather to show the error of accepting a tradition over scriptural truth. If we do get carried away by tradition, we jeopardize our faith and open doors to our soul that could be detrimental to our relationship with God. When speaking of religion, in this book I refer to the system that has been set in place, and not necessarily all the people that have membership in such a group.

The following pages contain what I believe to be a true understanding of a truth already revealed in

Scripture. I have asked the question of myself and others in countless conversations through the years; how is it that we can read Scripture for years and not always see what is revealed?

The subject of this book is one such portion of scripture that seems to stay hidden in spite of the Scripture being very plain in its treatment of this most important and precious truth. I have come to the conclusion that it is simply a problem as old as man. We have a very difficult time giving up our traditions, even if they have no basis in truth or Scripture. This has been true since men began to form societies and religions, whether Christian or pagan in nature. Even in the secular world change comes with great reluctance. The great explorers were laughed at when they asserted the earth was round and not flat as it was believed to be at the time. Even today, with pictures from space, there still remains a flat earth society. The great inventors were often scorned and misunderstood because their ideas broke with traditional ways of doing things. The great artists were seldom revered in their lifetimes. Only after they were long dead did people see the skill and genius of their work.

I hope you will read this book with an open mind for it is not my intention to tear anything down, but to reveal a deeper spiritual truth that will cause your walk with Jesus to be greater than ever before.

Robert A. French

Chapter One

"RITUALS, CEREMONIES, & SYMBOLISM"

In order to understand how traditions evolve in societies, let's first look at the definition of one of the words. Since ceremony, ritual and imagery all have their existence in tradition; we will only need to look at the following word.

***Tradition**, from the Greek word "paradosis" meaning; transmission, that is, (concretely) a precept; specifically the Jewish traditionary law: ordinance, tradition. (Strong's #3862)*[1]

By this definition, we see that a tradition is passed down orally from generation to generation. No matter what the religion might be; Christian or pagan, a tradition almost always involves some sort of ceremony or observance. In Jewish tradition, which is what we are concerned with here, it was always a ceremony, a sacrifice or solemn gathering of the tribes according to God's command. As long as these ceremonies were observed in the spirit in which they were intended, there was no problem. However, the two had to go together. The spirit, or the real meaning which the ceremony was made to represent, had to be remembered and incorporated into the ritual by the people or it had no meaning. This is the great weakness of traditional religious rites. Their meaning tends to get lost as they are told and retold to each successive generation. This is a basic weakness in this form of worship and was only intended for a period of time until the Messiah Jesus would be revealed to the world.

Man by his very nature, is a visual creature. You have heard the saying; "a picture is worth a thousand words." In the modern world, we are bombarded every day from every direction with visual stimulation. When many people are asked if they have read a certain book, they will say; "no, but I saw the movie." However, we all know that even when dealing with a subject based in fact, movie makers take a lot of license with the material and in many cases it does not resemble what actually took place. Therefore, if we were to depend solely upon the movie industry for our historical education, I'm afraid we would have a much skewed view of our past. In the course of my work, I have by necessity, dealt with many people in the advertising industry. I have never had any of them suggest to me to use more text than pictures. In fact, it is just the opposite.

We also carry this visual trait over into our religious life. Why read the Bible when we can just perform a ritual or look at a statue? After all, the Bible is a big book and it is too hard to understand; also, it's written in that old English which I just can't get into. It is very easy for us to get into the pomp and pageantry of ritualistic religious ceremony and never really understand what God actually intended for us. When you inquire of most laymen who are members of highly ritualistic religions about what they believe, you generally get a very general overview of their church. In my personal experience, they usually know very little about the Bible and when challenged become irritated or try to change the subject. Often they will direct you to their ministers claiming they are the ones who have biblical understanding and they are the ones who are entrusted with their spiritual welfare. This was a failing in Israel in the Old Testament. Even though they had a system of priests that took care of the temple, God still held all of Israel responsible for knowing and keeping the Law of Moses. If they found themselves in disfavor with God, they could not blame the priests or claim ignorance of God's law. They were held accountable. Because of this, I think it is a dangerous thing to trust your eternal soul to a minister or priest or religious organization when according to New Testament Scripture each of us when we stand before God will give an account of our own lives and will be judged accordingly. *For there is one God and one mediator between God and men, the man Christ Jesus.* (1 Tim. 2:5 NIV)

Many ritualistic religious ceremonies began in Christianity simply because the people didn't understand what was being said to them at the time. Jesus was always wondering at the lack of understanding of his disciples, when after speaking a parable, they would come to him asking the meaning. This has been a problem with man since the beginning. When presented with higher spiritual concepts, he looks down to the natural things around him to explain what he doesn't really understand. This is why all the pagan religions carved idols out of stone or other materials, because they could not grasp the concept of God. In the book of Romans Paul refers to this. *Although they claimed to be wise, they became fools and exchanged the glory of the immortal God for images made to look like mortal man and birds and animals and reptiles.* (Rom. 1:22-23 NIV) It seems that we cannot get ourselves to any higher plain, but what we can see with our natural eyes.

There is one trait that all the great men of God had in common. They could all see beyond the natural world around them. They did not have any need of the natural things around them to worship or know their God. They were able to by faith; see another realm hidden from other men. Hidden, not because it was forbidden to them, but because their spiritual senses were dulled by not having faith in anything but what they could see in the natural world. Hebrews Chapter Eleven is a testament to just a few, who by faith, overcame the limitations of their natural sight, and saw into the realm of the spirit and because of this received from God special favor. Abel, Enoch, Noah, Abraham and Sarah are mentioned here by the writer because they were able to see beyond this natural realm. Noah was able to believe God and know that it was going to rain even though he had never seen rain. Up until that time, it had never rained on the earth. Abraham was able by faith, to look down through the ages and

"Rituals, Ceremonies, & Symbolism"

---

see the city of God, confessing that he looked for a city whose builder and maker is God. Sarah was able by faith, to believe Gods promise even though she was past age to conceive and bear a child. Everything these people knew by their natural senses told them what they were expecting was not possible; but they had absolutely no doubt it would happen. They did all this strictly by FAITH. They did not need rituals; or ceremonies, or priests, or ministers, or images made by men. They did it because they knew God on a spiritual plane, not impeded by their natural senses. They believed what God had promised them, simply because He said it.

Rituals, ceremonies, imagery and traditions serve only to hide God from us. They're like the veil that was in the Holy of Holies that hid God from Israel. They are like the Law of Moses that while it provided some comfort to Israel, it never let them have a one on one personal relationship with God. We must not go back to the ritualistic ceremonial practices of the Old Testament, but rather go beyond the veil and worship God as Jesus instructed us in the book of John; *Yet a time is coming and has now come when the true worshipers will worship the Father in spirit and truth, for they are the kind of worshipers the Father seeks. God is a spirit, and his worshipers must worship in spirit and in truth.* (Jn 4:23 NIV)

Many of the ceremonies of the law have been carried over into the New Testament church by changing them slightly, but they were never intended to remain after Jesus came. Man, however, is a very stubborn creature and turning loose of old habits comes hard to his flesh. Even under the Old Covenant the rituals and ceremonies became a stench in the nostrils of God because the people had forgotten all about why they were doing them. In the first Chapter of the book of Isaiah, we find a strongly worded rebuke of Israel because their ceremonies and rituals had become the focal point of their religion, and not God himself. I heard a man say one time that "rules without relationship breeds rebellion." This is exactly what Israel had done. They had forgotten their relationship with God and no longer kept the law out of any love of God, but out of a self righteous piety used to gain position among the people. They made a pretense of keeping the law, but were in rebellion against God at the same time. *The multitude of your sacrifices— what are they to me?" says the LORD. "I have more than enough of burnt offerings, of rams and the fat of fattened animals; I have no pleasure in the blood of bulls and lambs and goats. When you come to appear before me, who has asked this of you, this trampling of my courts? Stop bringing meaningless offerings! Your incense is detestable to me. New Moons, Sabbaths and convocations— I cannot bear your evil assemblies. Your New Moon festivals and your appointed feasts my soul hates. They have become a burden to me; I am weary of bearing them.* (Isa. 1:11-14 NIV) Verses eleven thru fourteen are particularly interesting in that it seems there is a contradiction between what God is saying to Israel now, and what was given in the Law of Moses. Wasn't it Jehovah that commanded Israel to bring sacrifices and honor holy days and feast days? The Bible, however, does not contradict itself;

so what is the meaning of this strong rebuke? Why would God say these things to his people when they apparently were keeping the sacrifice and holy days and feast days? Because it is easy as time goes by, to get caught up in the sacraments of religion and forget the real reasons behind them. The sacraments of the law were only to continue until Jesus; such as animal sacrifice, Passover, and feast days. All of these were fulfilled in Jesus the Messiah.

For what the law was powerless to do in that it was weakened by the sinful nature God did by sending his own Son in the likeness of sinful man to be a sin offering. And so he condemned sin in sinful man. (Rom. 8:3 NIV) However, some of these rituals have been carried on in the Christian church of today with the same harmful effects they created under the law. We have changed them to fit into modern life and sometimes called them by different names but they are still just diluted versions of the same thing.

God, in my opinion, knew from the beginning that the law was not the answer for His plan of redemption for man, but just a stop gap measure until it was time for Jesus to come into the world. When we read of any of the men of renown in the Old Testament, we find one thing in common. They all had a very personal relationship with God which was based in their love of Him. They were not boasters of their own accomplishments and did not seek the adoration of men, but rather the approval of their God. The ones that had trouble pleasing God were those who kept the sacraments just for show, to bolster their own egos and be thought of as righteous men among the people. This latter condition is not as difficult to fall into as it seems when through time, all that is taught is the ceremonies and rituals of the religion. They were taught that all they had to do to please God was keep the law, but when there is no love of God applied and no heartfelt repentance before Him, it is difficult to keep. They kept the sacrifice, ceremonies, Sabbaths and feast days, but the true meaning of the law was forgotten. They forgot to treat each other fairly, to love their neighbor to care for the widows and orphans to not shed innocent blood to not bear false witness; in short they forgot most of the real meaning of the Law of Moses.

Chapter Two

"OLD COVENANT OR NEW"

In dealing with this subject we need to go to the very beginning, when God made man and put him in the garden to keep it. When God first made man, or, as the word translated here actually means, red earth or Adam; there was no religion or ritualistic ceremonies of any kind. There was only God and his creation. He gave Adam only one commandment, he was not to eat of the tree of the knowledge of good and evil. God put his trust in Adam to obey what he had told him to do, and set about to build their relationship by coming and talking to him in the cool of the day. Nothing else was needed to keep this relationship but obedience on Adam's part to what God had instructed him to do. This was the first state of grace for man and was what God intended from the beginning. There was no redemption needed and no law had been given to this innocent creation God had formed from the dust of the ground. All was good, until Adam made a choice that would, until Jesus the Messiah came, bring all men under condemnation because of sin. God had trusted him and now by partaking of what he had been told was forbidden, he broke his trust with his Creator. It is not necessary here to go into all the reasons Adam did what he did. It's sufficient for what we are discussing in this chapter to understand that because of the disobedience of this man, God was to redefine for several millennia, his relationship with the family of men. It will be a long time before Moses is asked to lead the chosen people out of Egypt to the land of promise, where they would dwell in peace and prosperity as long as they obeyed the law.

The question that begs to be asked at this point is this; was the law that came by Moses ever really intended, or was it just a stop-gap measure instituted, depending on what you did with it, as a form of punishment or of blessing? *In general, law is a rule of action prescribed for the government of rational beings or moral agents, to which rule they are bound to yield obedience, <u>in default of which they are exposed to punishment</u>* [Webster's unabridged dictionary][2] . The law can only do two things; it can expose you if you break it and punish you for the infraction. *For what the law was powerless to do in that it was weakened by the sinful nature, God did by sending his own Son in the likeness of sinful man to be a sin offering. And so he condemned sin in sinful man.* (Rom. 8:3 NIV) The law could not pardon sin, it could not sanctify the sinner, nor could it justify anyone before God. All it could do was to expose, judge and prescribe a punishment for breaking it. I have always been curious as to why God did not give the law to Adam, or to Noah or other men who were before Moses if it was intended from the beginning. It wasn't until the Israelites had rebelled in the wilderness that God called Moses to the mount and gave him the tablets. From Adam to Noah and the flood, there were many that lived in right relationship with God without any of the regulations that were later imposed on the nation of Israel. From this I can only conclude that the Law was not God's first choice, but because of Israel's rebelliousness, it was imposed on them. There were two reasons for the imposition of the Law. One, so that Israel could not plead ignorance in wrong doing, because the Law made it plain what was right and what was wrong putting the responsibility upon their own heads if they broke it. *What shall we say, then? Is the law sin? Certainly not! Indeed I would not have known what sin was except through the law. For I would not have known what coveting really was if the law had not said, "Do not covet.* (Rom. 7:7 NIV) Two, it was given as types and shadows to show us Jesus and what was really intended from the beginning. When Jesus came, what was intended from the foundation of the world was fulfilled by the sacrifice of His body and blood.

We only need to examine the third chapter of Genesis to see the first work of God's grace toward his creation when Adam and Eve partook of the fruit of the tree of knowledge and became aware that they were naked, they hid themselves and sewed fig leaves together and made aprons to cover their nakedness. When God came in the cool of the day to visit with Adam, he found him hiding in the bushes and asked him why he was hiding. Adam replied that he was hiding because he was naked. God then asked him who told him he was naked and the story unfolds. I will not here include all the text because of space but you can read it in Genesis, the third Chapter. I know there are many who might find what I am about to say controversial, but this is the first example of grace found in scripture. God had told Adam and Eve that if they disobeyed and ate of the Tree of Knowledge, they would surly die. However, the fact is, they did not die. God did not bring judgment on them at that time. It could be speculated that God intended to destroy them on the spot as he did others in Scripture that disobeyed, but changed His mind because of His great love and compassion. However, He still imposed the sentence of death because of the transgression, and man's appointment with death was established. However, there is something greater that happened at this time that forever changed God's intended purpose for man. In order to understand what transpired in the Garden we need to look at what God did right at that time. When God found them, they had already made for themselves aprons out of fig leaves. Why was this not sufficient for them? What did it matter anyway, if God had imposed on them the sentence of death? But instead, God made them clothes out of the skins of an animal and covered them. My question is, where did God get the skins and what did he have to do to get them? He had to kill an animal and shed its blood. I believe this was the first example of sacrifice for sin or disobedience, and even though God was very grieved he showed his great capacity for love and forgiveness. It is said later in Scripture that, without the shedding of blood there is no forgiveness. (Heb. 9:22 NIV) I am firmly convinced that the doctrine of Grace is not exclusively a New Testament teaching. The idea of Grace was born in the heart of God that day in the Garden where it all began, and the plan for man's ultimate redemption was set in motion. Somehow, Adam was made to understand this and later, even though it is not written, explained the principle to his sons, Cain and Abel. Adam was made to know that the sacrifice was not as important as the meaning behind it, and that it was the great love and mercy of God that gave it meaning.

When Cain and Abel brought their first offering to the Lord, they understood the principal they had been taught. If all that matters is that we bring a sacrifice, then why was Abel accepted and Cain rejected? Their offerings were both of the first fruits of their labors, which was acceptable in the sight of God. Part of the reason might have been that Abel's offering was a sin offering, that is to say it required the slaying of a sheep, thereby shedding blood. However, I really think it had more to do with the attitude of Cain's heart than anything else. God does not want our sacrifice or ritual or ceremonies, he wants our hearts. *For I desire mercy not sacrifice; and the acknowledgement of God rather than burnt offerings.* (Hos. 6:6 NIV) There is a great difference between faith based in love and ritualistic religion based in law.

From Adam to Moses, there were men who walked with God without the benefit of the law or prescribed rituals. How did they do this without any written instruction or manuals to go by? In fact, one of these men pleased God so much that he was taken by the Lord and did not see death. His name was Enoch, and according to Genesis 5: 23-24; he only lived to be 365 years of age, a relatively young man for his day, then he was no more for God took him away. (NIV) The writer of Hebrews refers to him in the eleventh Chapter of the book along with many others that by faith, walked with God. It doesn't say that by the law or by sacrifice or ritual they walked with God, but rather by faith.

The rituals, ceremonies, and symbolism of the Old Covenant were never intended to be carried over into the New Covenant. What Jesus did by his death, burial and resurrection forever fulfilled the Law and the prophets, and brought to us a more pure form of worship and closer relationship with him than had ever been known before.

Jesus declared, *Believe me, woman, a time is coming when you will worship the Father neither on this mountain nor in Jerusalem. You Samaritans worship what you do not know; we worship what we do know, for salvation is from the Jews. Yet a time is coming and has now come when the true worshipers will worship the Father in spirit and truth, for they are the kind of worshipers the Father seeks. God is spirit and his worshipers must worship in spirit and in truth*. (Jn. 4:21-24 NIV) This was a revolutionary statement by our Lord. He was saying that no longer would people have to come to a certain place or build altars, but they could worship anywhere they were. They no longer needed the natural or man-made temples, or rituals, or ceremonies, but rather the altar of their heart. The weakness of the law was that as it was told to generation after generation, it lost its real meaning and became just a set of rules. Rules without relationship will cause rebellion as it did in the people of Israel. As time went by, each succeeding generation became dull of hearing and their eyes could not see as their fathers had in the desert, or when they crossed over into the land of promise. We are the same today. How many young people today have deep seated feelings about World War II? How many show emotion or passion when talking about it? However, when speaking to a veteran about the war, often their eyes fill with tears and they choke with passion when sharing their experiences with others. Why is this? It is because they experienced it first-hand and it was not just something they read in a book, or someone told them about. Most Christian Religions talk about a Jesus who died on a cross two thousand years ago. They see him on a cross bleeding and dying and in certain places they picture him dead. I have seen Christ portrayed by life-size statues dead and lying in glass coffins for the people to pass by or to pray to. It is hard to relate to or stay passionate about something that happened two thousand years ago that you never saw or participated in. To all too many religions, it's just a great story about a great teacher that has been passed down from generation to generation; but the real meaning and passion has not come along with it. Rites, rituals and ceremonies can be done without passion, or love, or faith, but real Christianity cannot. The Scriptures tell us; *Therefore, brothers, since we have confidence to enter the Most Holy Place by the blood of Jesus, by a new and living way opened for us through the curtain, that is, his body, and since we have a great priest over the house of God, let us draw near to God with a sincere heart in full assurance of faith, having our hearts sprinkled to cleanse us from a guilty conscience and having our bodies washed with pure water. Let us hold unswervingly to the hope we profess, for he who promised is faithful.* (Heb. 10:19-23 NIV) Jesus is not dead, he is not on a cross and he is not just a great man that lived long ago. He is not worshiped or served through rites, rituals or ceremonies but in a new and living way by those who have come to know him as he is, alive and sitting at the right hand of the father making intercession for those who walk by faith and not by sight.

Chapter Three

"WHAT DOES IT MATTER"

(Hebrews 9:8-15)

Verse 8: The Holy Spirit was showing by this that the way into the Most Holy Place had not yet been disclosed as long as the first tabernacle was still standing. Verse 9: This is an illustration for the present time, indicating that the gifts and sacrifices being offered were not able to clear the conscience of the worshiper. Verse 10: They are only a matter of food and drink and various ceremonial washings—external regulations applying until the time of the new order. 11. When Christ came as high priest of the good things that are already here, he went through the greater and more perfect tabernacle that is not man-made, that is to say, not a part of this creation. Verse 12: He did not enter by means of the blood of goats and calves; but he entered the Most Holy Place once for all by his own blood, having obtained eternal redemption. Verse 13: The blood of goats and bulls and the ashes of a heifer sprinkled on those who are ceremonially

unclean sanctify them so that they are outwardly clean. Verse 14: How much more, then, will the blood of Christ, who through the eternal Spirit offered himself unblemished to God, cleanse our consciences from acts that lead to death, so that we may serve the living God! Verse 15: For this reason Christ is the mediator of a new covenant, that those who are called may receive the promised eternal inheritance—now that he has died as a ransom to set them free from the sins committed under the first covenant. (NIV)

The name of this chapter reflects the question I am always asked. What does it matter if we continue the ceremonies and rituals in a strictly symbolic form? And my answer is always, a great deal in every way. As in Verse 8 of the texts quoted above while the first tabernacle was still standing the way into the New Covenant was still hidden. In other words it was not possible to enter into the New Covenant while the ordinances of the first tabernacle, the Law of Moses, were still being practiced. Verse 10 tells us that the old ordinances were only valid until the new order which was the New Covenant that came by Jesus the Christ. Based upon these Scriptures I must conclude that <u>As long as we keep establishing the Old Covenant in our lives we cannot fully receive the benefit of the New Covenant as it cannot be fully disclosed.</u> In order to understand this more fully we must separate the Law of Moses into two parts. The first being the Ten Commandments Scripture reference found in Exodus 20. The second part being the ordinances which include the sacrifices, ceremonial washings, feast days, Sabbaths, Passover, punishments, etc. The Ten

Commandments were the foundation of God's intent of how we were to relate to him, denoted by the first four and how we were to relate to our fellow man denoted by the last six. The second part of the law which was supposed to be based on the Ten Commandants; for the sake of understanding, I will separate into three parts. The first being the sacrifices that were to be offered for sin and various other reasons at different times. The second being the celebrations of the law such as Passover, Feast days and Sabbaths, which were days to commemorate the things God had done. Thirdly, were the punishments set out for violations of the law.

For the sake of understanding, let's think of the first Covenant as the original will that God made for his people. Then think of the New Covenant as a codicil to the original will. A codicil is a supplement to a will whereby the original is changed or amended. It doesn't do away with the first will but amends or updates it as to things that may have changed since it was originally written. This makes easy understanding of Jesus words; *Do not think that I have come to abolish the Law or the Prophets; I have not come to abolish them but to fulfill them. I tell you the truth, until heaven and earth disappear, not the smallest letter, not the least stroke of a pen, will by any means disappear from the Law until everything is accomplished. Anyone who breaks one of the least of these <u>commandments</u> and teaches others to do the same will be called least in the kingdom of heaven, but whoever practices and teaches these commands will be called great in the kingdom of heaven.* (Matt. 5:17-19 NIV) We see in this portion of Scripture, the only part of the law

Jesus refers to are the Commandments. He does not refer to the keeping of sacrifices or ceremonies but simply the Commandments. In (Mark 10:17-21) we find a reference to a man who asked Jesus what he must do to be saved. Jesus did not ask him if he had gone to the temple to make sacrifice, or if he had kept the Passover, or if he kept the Feast days. He asked him if he had kept the Commandments and the man answered that he had since he was a child. Notice that the Commandments were the only thing that Jesus asked about, because they were the only thing still pertinent to the will that was already in the process of being changed. The will itself is still intact, but Jesus, the codicil, has forevermore changed the way it is to be administered. The very moment Jesus was born; God's perfect plan for redemption was set in motion. All that had come before was just a precursor, types and shadows of what was really intended.

The second part of the law which was the ordinances by which it was administered, was what the codicil amended. Jesus Himself being the codicil, just as he was the veil or curtain in the temple. The Commandments would now be administered by a grace system instead of a law of works. Salvation being a gift you could not earn by works, but was rather given as a gift to those who came to Jesus, in faith, and repented their sins. Now we can understand some of Jesus actions that were against what the law said to do. This explains Paul's teachings about Law and grace. We can understand the many rebukes made by Jesus to the Pharisees and Sadducees and keepers of the law. Examples are found in Mark 7:2-23 when

Jesus' disciples were accused by the Pharisees of eating with unwashed hands. Also in Matthew 12:1 the Pharisees accused the disciples of doing that which was not lawful on the Sabbath day, picking and eating corn. In Mark 3:2 they sought to accuse Him of healing the sick on the Sabbath. In all these instances he either said something that they could not answer or he rebuked them sternly. He was not objecting to the Commandments but the ordinances of the law that had been fulfilled by his coming and their hypocrisy.

Notice what the end of Matthew 5:13 (NIV) says *"But to fulfill them"* or better said he was literally the fulfillment of the law. The word fulfill used here means to cram full or to end a thing. Full to the point that it will hold no more, therefore bringing it to an end. The law given by Moses was only a precursor of the true plan of God that would be fulfilled in Jesus the Christ. The law had done all that it ever could or was intended to do, being full to the brim. We would no longer need to shed the blood of animals on altars of stone, or observe feast days and other rituals of the law, but we would now be able to see God in the person of Jesus as he became the sacrifice once and for all. *Philip said, "Lord, show us the Father and that will be enough for us. Jesus answered: "Don't you know me, Philip, even after I have been among you such a long time? <u>Anyone who has seen me has seen the Father.</u> How can you say, 'Show us the Father?"* (Jn 14:8-9 NIV) Jesus never intended to do away with the spirit of the law or the true meaning, but he did do away with the rituals and ceremonies contained therein, as they were no longer valid. Religion has never been able to completely do away with the tradition, ritual and ceremonies, but rather, in point of fact, have created new ones said to resemble the old but are simply symbolic.

Chapter Four

"THE PASSOVER"
(Exodus 12)

For the sake of understanding, we need to have knowledge of the ordinance of Passover, according to the Law of Moses. We need to know why it was instituted and what its significance was to the nation of Israel. First, let us see why it was instituted by looking at the event that brought it about.

In the book of Exodus 12 beginning at the first verse, we find the account of this great event. It is to commemorate the last plague that God visited on Egypt, just before the Exodus of the children of Israel from that land. This was the death of all the firstborn of Egypt, from Pharaoh to the lowest slave, and also the firstborn of the cattle. (Para. Ex. 11:4-6 NIV) To protect all the families of Israel from this terrible plague, Moses commanded the head of each household to sacrifice a lamb and to take a hyssop and sprinkle the blood of the sacrifice on the sides and tops of the door frames of their houses. When the destroyer came, he would see the blood on the door posts and pass over that house, sparing the firstborn from death. (Para. Ex. 12:12-13 NIV) This is the event the Passover was to commemorate.

Exodus 12: beginning at the fourteenth verse gives us the details of how this ordinance of the Passover was to be celebrated. It took place in the month of Abib or Nisan, which corresponds to our April, beginning on the evening of the fourteenth day of the month, until the evening of the twenty first day of the month. I will only concern myself here with the major components of this festival that are pertinent to our subject. The sacrifice was to be a lamb, one for each household. If there were not enough persons in the family they were allowed to invite others to share with them so that all of the lamb would be eaten. None of it was allowed to remain until the next day. The animals had to be male and could be taken from the sheep or goats of their flocks. They also had to be a year old. All the people of the community of Israel had to slay the animals at twilight, then take some of the blood and sprinkle it on the door posts of their houses. They were to eat the sacrifice with bitter herbs and unleavened bread, and if any of the sacrifice was left over they were to burn it so nothing remained until the next day. They also were to eat unleavened bread for seven days and to remove all yeast from their houses during this time. These are the major components of the feast of Passover. It was later refined in areas by Moses to accommodate problems of distance and certain other things that I will not go into at this time. However, I will say that in the modern world, the Passover is celebrated in no

"The Passover"

---

way as it was in ancient Israel for reasons that should be obvious to the reader.

As I have stated in earlier in this book the Old Covenant is merely a type and shadow of the New Covenant that was to come. Just as grace has always been the true heart of God, these festivals and ceremonies were simply images in which the truth was hidden, to be revealed in Gods time. The Passover is probably the greatest example of this. It really becomes prophetical in that it perfectly describes the Lamb that was slain before the foundations of the world. These were not just ritualistic festivals and ceremonies, but images of things that would come and change forever the relationship of God with men.

The first component to examine in this festival is the sacrificial lamb. This sacrifice speaks of deliverance from bondage that Israel had suffered for over four hundred years. It speaks to salvation from a cruel system that decimated the people of Israel and kept them from their land and their God. This is a type of Jesus and what his sacrifice accomplished for whosoever would come to him and believe unto salvation.

The eating of unleavened bread for seven days is also significant in that it reveals how precious his word is to us. Leaven or yeast raises bread dough so that it becomes lighter and more tender to the palate. However, in order to do this, it acts on the sugars in the flour, thereby changing the structure of the bread. This process changes the structure, texture and taste of the bread altering it from its original form. This is done all too often to the word of God. By the time it gets to the hearer it is unrecognizable from its original intent. Jesus refers to this when he chastised the Pharisees. *Be careful, Jesus said to them. Be on your guard against the yeast of the Pharisees and Sadducees.* (Matt. 16:6 NIV) The word "bread" is used symbolically throughout Scripture. Jesus used this symbolism when he said to his disciples, *I am the living bread that came down from heaven. If anyone eats of this bread, he will live forever. This bread is my flesh, which I will give for the life of the world.* (Jn. 6:5 NIV) I will discuss this at length in a later chapter. We see then that the unleavened bread is a representation of the living word that was to come and that word was Jesus. The third component is the time of year the Passover was held. To the casual reader this might go unnoticed but it has real meaning. Jesus was born about the time of Passover according to Scripture, not in December, as most of the world seems to think. It's significant because all parts of this festival had to relate to Jesus, and as we see, they do. If the Passover was intended to be kept in any form, then it should be done as it was then. Nothing should be changed in the festival at all. It should not be some watered down version or some spiritualized option as some suppose it is. My contention is that it wasn't meant to be kept as it was and not, as some suppose, to keep it today. It is to be understood as a type and shadow of the truth that was to come in the Person of Jesus the Christ. In the following chapters, I will show how this most beautiful of all symbolism, The Passover, is really to be celebrated in the New Testament church.

Chapter Five

"SACRAMENT OF COMMUNION AN EXAMINATION OF THE WORD"

To fully understand the meaning of this word and how it is used in the New Testament let us look at the Greek word from which it is translated. The following is from Strong's Exhaustive Concordance.

κοινωνία koinōnia
koy-nohn-ee'-ah

From G2844; partnership, that is, (literally) participation, or (social) intercourse, or (pecuniary) benefaction:–(to) communicate (-ation), communion, (contri-), distribution, fellowship.³

By the Catholic and Eastern Orthodox churches, it is called the Eucharist or Holy Communion. In most Protestant churches it is simply communion, and in some, Holy Communion. It only varies in what is meant by the term "communion". In the Catholic and Eastern Orthodox churches, the doctrine is *transubstantiation,* which teaches that the elements literally transform into the flesh and blood of Jesus when eaten and drunk. In the Protestant churches it is taught as just symbolically representing the body and blood of the Lord Jesus. I have come to believe through my study of Scripture that both of the aforementioned doctrines are in error. In the following chapter, I will go into detail why I have come to that conclusion, but let me first lay a little foundation as to the history of this most sacred rite of the church–Catholic, Orthodox and Protestant.

First, let us look at the word itself and its meaning. You may think I am nitpicking but I believe words mean what they convey to the reader or hearer, and can mislead the reader or hearer into misconceptions that can be detrimental to their spiritual life and growth. I have placed the definition of communion at the beginning of this chapter according to Strong's Concordance of the Bible. In this definition there is nothing said about eating or drinking or transformation. It is not just fellowship or friendship, but is a literal participation in Christ. It speaks to the exchange of thoughts or ideas and agreement between two or more parties. It takes us away from the carnal realm and places us into the community of faith, which is his body. How is this accomplished? It is done by speaking or reading or even sign language, but never through eating or drinking. You may converse or read while enjoying a repast, however, you are not communing unless you are in conversation with those around you. It is my contention, that if you were only to take the elements of the communion and never heard or read anything Jesus said; you would know nothing of him and the taking of the elements would be of no benefit to you whatsoever. For example; if you never heard that Jesus said "repent" you would not know to do it. If you never heard the beatitudes of Jesus, you would not know he blessed the poor, merciful, meek, etc. Had he never spoken or taught us who he is, we would never have known he was ever here. He would have been treated as a carpenter that went about his daily chores as everyone else, and would have passed into history unknown without having fulfilled his mission. He had to communicate the kingdom of God to us with words, or we would not have known it. To commune is to communicate in some form so as to be understood by those around us. Jesus had communion everyday with his disciples and the throngs who came to hear him by his words. His words were so unique and powerful that it was said of him; *No one ever spoke the way this man does, the guards declared.* (Jn. 7:46 NIV) It was his words that forever more changed the face of the world. The church at large today puts more stock in their rites, rituals and ceremonies than they do in what Jesus said. In point of fact, most people who attend a church of any kind know little of the Bible and its teachings. Quotes like; "cleanliness is next to Godliness, and you shall not kill" are commonly thought to be from the Bible but this is not the case. The first quote is not there at all and the latter quote is a misinterpretation of Scripture. The Commandant does not say; you shall not kill, but rather, thou shall not commit murder.

There is a distinct difference between the two. This is why ignorant and unlearned men claim there are so many contradictions in the Bible. They have no understanding and they do not care to. As the Church, however, we feed their ignorance by our misquoting Scripture and by not applying logic to our argument. Let's examine the statement; "You shall not kill. (Exodus 20:13) The NIV translates it correctly; "you shall not murder." [râtsach raw-tsakh'] "A primitive root; properly to dash in pieces, that is, kill (a human being), <u>especially to murder:</u>–put to death, kill, (man-) slay (-er), murder (-er)." (Strong's)[4] The Hebrew says kill in a general sense, but specifically murder, and murder is the sense given in this verse. W.E. Vine gives a more complete understanding; "rashach (H7523), "to kill, murder, slay." This verb occurs more than forty times in the Old Testament, and its concentration is in the Pentateuch. Rashach is rare in Rabbinic Hebrew, and its usage has been increased in <u>modern Hebrew with the exclusive meaning of "to murder."</u> [5] There is a difference. If "You shall not kill" is correct, then Saul and David were the grossest of men because the women sang songs about them saying; Saul has slain his thousands and David his ten thousands.[6] And yet, God said of David "he is a man after my own heart." Unlearned men will say, See? I told you the Bible is full of contradictions", but they would be wrong. You see, God never said anywhere you could not defend yourself or your nation. He just said you were not to murder anyone, to kill without just cause. The greatest example of this I know of is in the New Testament. Jesus is about to be taken into custody by those who accused him and when a servant of the High Priest stepped forward, Peter, a disciple of Jesus, drew his sword and cut off the man's ear.[7] The question is, why was Peter carrying a sword in the first place? I don't know how we read the Bible and completely overlook these things. It is interesting to note that Jesus did not tell Peter to get rid of his sword, but to put it back in its sheath. He evidently had no problem with Peter carrying a sword. Jesus did not go into a righteous tirade about how Peter could possibly be his disciple and carry a weapon. I wonder what would have happened had Jesus not communicated with Peter what his wishes were. Would Peter have continued his attack on the servant in his attempt to save his Lord? Suffice it to say we need to rightly divide the word of truth if we are going to be the Christians God wants us to be. In the book of Luke 22:36, we find Jesus' instruction to his disciples; *He said to them, "But now if you have a purse take it, and also a bag; and if you don't have a sword, sell your cloak and buy one.* (NIV) In true fact, all of the followers of Jesus that night were armed with swords, according to Luke. Verses forty-nine and fifty speak to this fact. *"When Jesus' followers saw what was going to happen, they said, "Lord, should we strike with our swords?" And one of them struck the servant of the high priest, cutting off his right ear.* (Luke 22:49-50 NIV) Jesus said to them, "this is not what I want", and healed the man's ear. The understanding of this was communicated to Pilate when Jesus was brought before him. *Jesus said, "My kingdom is not of this world. If it were, my servants would fight to prevent my arrest by the Jews. But now my kingdom is from another place."* (John 18:36 NIV) They did not carry their weapons for offensive purposes but rather for protection from wild beasts and robbers, etc. This however, debunks the notion that as Christians, we never have the right to defend ourselves. It is imperative that as Christians, we understand what the truth of the Scripture is. I gave these examples to show how easy it is to misconstrue or be misled as to the real meaning of Scripture compared to what is taught by many, in the religious world today.

True communion with Jesus is not found in rites, rituals or ceremonies but in his word. It's more important to hear his voice and be taught than it is to sup with him. I personally do not believe in the doctrine of transubstantiation, nor do I believe we need a watered down version. It is not what Jesus intended or meant when he said; Take eat; this is my body and drink for this is my blood. (Matt.26:26 NIV) In the next chapter of this book I will deal with what I believe to be the single most astounding revelation of Jesus in the entire Bible. It's more astounding because it came from his lips. He was the one who was doing the talking.

Chapter Six

"An Examination of John 6"

The narrative I will concern myself with in John 6, is the greatest revelation that Jesus ever gave us about himself. He reveals to us his person, his will and how, as mere human beings we can enter into the kingdom of God by and through him. Let those that read this, have ears to hear and hearts open to receive what Jesus is saying to the Church.

Just before Jesus gave those who were there that day this great revelation of himself; he had preformed two wondrous miracles. The first was the feeding of the multitude with a boy's lunch of five loaves of barley bread and two small fish. His disciples departed from that place by ship, crossing the Sea of Galilee to Capernaum. After they had rowed a few miles, Jesus came to them walking on the sea, and when he entered the boat it was immediately at land. When those who had been fed found that Jesus had departed to Capernaum, they went to him there to see what he would say to them. Now the reason he had departed secretly, was because Jesus had perceived they were going to force him into being their king, insomuch as this was not his mission, He sought no earthly crowns, He slipped away. When they came to him they said "Rabbi, when did you come here?" *Jesus answered them and said, "Most assuredly, I say to you, you seek Me, not because you saw the signs, but because you ate of the loaves and were filled. Do not labor for the food which perishes, but for the food which endures to everlasting life, which the Son of Man will give you, because God the Father has set His seal on Him."* (Jn. 6:26-27 NIV) Here, we see a classic example of the darkness in the minds of carnal men. They could not see any farther than the fact that he had fed them and their desire to have a king who would lead them against the Roman Empire, for the purpose of delivering Israel from Roman tyranny. Why had they totally misunderstood his message? Because they were listening for what they wanted him to say and not what he was saying. For example: if a class of students were listening to a teacher expound on some rule of math or science, they would, in order to understand, have to pay close attention to what he was saying, shutting out any preconceived ideas or notions of their own. If they were not able to discipline their minds in such a manner, they would no doubt fail the course.

Jesus came at a time when Israel was in great conflict. The Roman Empire had spread its influence to the Middle East, where they had become ruler over Palestine. The Jews secretly were planning how they might revolt against Rome and free their land from Roman rule. We need to understand the Rabbis' idea

"An Examination of John 6"

of Messiah, was that of another David to sit on the throne of Israel; a warrior king to deliver them from their enemies. We have Scriptural proof of this fact, found in the book of John chapter 6:15; *Jesus, knowing that they intended to come and <u>make him king by force,</u> withdrew again to a mountain by himself.* (NIV) At first, when Jesus came doing miracles, they thought even though some were dubious of him; he might be the one prophesied to come. With his obvious power, surely he would have been able to vanquish the Romans and end their rule over the land of Israel. When by Jesus' own words, it became obvious this was not his purpose, they stopped hearing what he was saying, and when they did deign to listen to him, it was only to hopefully hear what they wanted him to say. I only refer to these things to show the carnality of the minds of the people at the time these things were taking place. It is easy to miss the true meaning of Jesus teachings when we are dull of hearing. I will here cite three examples that make very clear the lack of understanding even among those who were closest to him. Phillip, a disciple of Jesus who should have understood Jesus words, evidently did not, as we see in the narrative found in John 14:5-9. *Thomas said to him, "Lord, we don't know where you are going, so how can we know the way?" Jesus answered, "I am the way and the truth and the life. No one comes to the Father except through me. If you really knew me, you would know my Father as well. From now on, you do know him and have seen him." Phillip said, "Lord, show us the Father and that will be enough for us" Jesus answered: Don't you know me, Phillip, even after*

I have been among you such a long time? Anyone who has seen me has seen the Father. How can you say, Show us the Father?" (NIV) Phillip evidently didn't even know who he had been following all this time, and he was a disciple. In Luke 8:5-10, we read about a parable Jesus spoke to the people that day. Afterward, His disciples asked him what the parable meant. In verses nine and ten, Jesus gives an explanation. *His disciples asked him what this parable meant. He said, "the knowledge of the secrets of the kingdom of God has been given to you, but to others I speak in parables, so that, though seeing, they may not see; though hearing, they may not understand."* (NIV) Even though they walked with him on a daily basis, they still had to have everything explained to them in private and even then, some still did not understand. The last example is found in Matthew 17:1-5; these verses speak of when Jesus was transfigured before Peter, James and John on the mount. Moses and Elijah appear speaking with Jesus. Peter, in his zeal makes a recommendation that three tabernacles should be erected, one for each Moses, Elijah and Jesus. In the fifth verse, God speaks out of the heavens saying; *"This is my son, whom I love: with him I am well pleased. Listen to him!"* (NIV) How like carnal men to completely misunderstand what they hear and see. Peter should have been listening closely rather than letting his mind run to erecting monuments that serve no purpose. He couldn't see the real importance of what was happening; he was too busy being religious. As the saying goes, he couldn't see the forest for the trees. Peter was observing a miraculous event, and instead of being attentive to what was being said, as the Scripture says they were speaking with each other, he was caught up in building monuments. God, showing his displeasure, spoke out of heaven telling Peter to listen to what was being spoken. Men haven't changed all that much down through the ages. We still seem to be more concerned about the tabernacles and cathedrals than what is being said in them. And sad to say, not even what is being said in many of them resembles the Gospel of Jesus. It's easy to see how He was misunderstood, even by those who were his closest associates. This is why, when most people are asked what they believe as regarding their faith or religion; they have great difficulty in elucidating even the basic tenets. Yet when asked where they attend church or what faith they adhere to, can readily give directions to a building and state the name of the particular denomination. They can also readily explain the different ceremonies and rituals that are practiced within their faith or religion but can seldom tell you the theology behind them.

In order to understand Jesus's discourse in the sixth Chapter of John we must first understand the terms He was using in symbolic language. The most explicit explanation is found in John Chapter One where it states; *In the beginning was the Word, and the Word was with God, and the Word was God. He was with God in the beginning. Through him all things were made; without him nothing was made that has been made. In him was life, and that life was the light of men. The light shines in the darkness, but the darkness has not understood it.* (John 1:1-5) (NIV) Skipping to the fourteenth verse we read; *The Word became flesh and made his dwelling among us. We have seen his glory, the glory of the One and Only, who came from the Father, full of grace and truth.* (John 1:14 NIV) In the beginning, the Word was that part of the trinity that was given power to by speaking, bring the worlds into existence. It was the instrument used for creation. He was, if you will, the voice of the Godhead whereby the will of God was created or brought into reality. When he came to earth in flesh form during the occupation of the Holy Land by the Roman Empire, he did exactly the same thing he had always done; he spoke Gods will into existence. He fulfilled the Law or, more properly, the first covenant and the prophets. He spoke into existence the New Covenant that would replace the Old Covenant with his death on the cross. This covenant was made between the Godhead for God said; *When God made his promise to Abraham, since there was no one greater for him to swear by, he swore by himself.* (Heb. 6:13 NIV) We read in another place in Paul's letter to the Galatians, a further explanation to what he said in Hebrews; *Brothers, let me take an example from everyday life. Just as no one can set aside or add to a human covenant that has been duly established, so it is in this case. The promises were spoken to Abraham and to his seed. The Scripture does not say "and to seeds," meaning many people, but "and to your seed," meaning one person, who is Christ. What I mean is this: The law, introduced 430 years later, does not set aside the covenant previously established by God and thus do away with the promise. For if the inheritance depends on the law, then it no longer depends on a promise; but God in his grace gave it to Abraham through a promise. What, then, was the purpose of the law? It was added because of transgressions until the Seed to whom the promise referred had come. The law was put into effect through angels by a mediator.*

A mediator, however, does not represent just one party; but God is one. (Gal 3:15-20 NIV) It is evident by this reference that Jesus was the intended seed of Abraham and that through Him would all the nations of the earth be blessed.

Let's examine what Jesus said in this Chapter that made many of his disciples turn from him and follow him no more. *So they asked him, "What miraculous sign then will you give that we may see it and believe you? What will you do? Our forefathers ate the manna in the desert; as it is written: 'He gave them bread from heaven to eat.'" Jesus said to them, "I tell you the truth, it is not Moses who has given you the bread from heaven, but it is my Father who gives you the true bread from heaven. For the bread of God is he who comes down from heaven and gives life to the world." "Sir," they said, "from now on give us this bread."* (John 6:30-34 NIV) Do we really believe that Jesus is a loaf of bread or a crushed cracker or a Eucharist wafer? Do we really believe it transforms into the body of the Lord Jesus as the doctrine of transubstantiation teaches? My question is, if it doesn't then what value is there in eating it? It does me no good whatsoever. On the other hand, if I do it symbolically, it still does me no service any more than the symbols of the law did for Israel. In the forgoing verses, Jesus starts his discourse with an answer to the question asked by those who examined him, who quoted from the Old Testament referring to the Manna that was given to Israel in the desert. They declared that the Manna was the bread of heaven but Jesus refuted this by saying he was the bread that came down from heaven. The Manna was not the bread of heaven but a natural substance, even though it came from God. By the description given, it was like coriander seed and looked like resin that was gathered and baked or boiled before eaten. *When the dew was gone, thin flakes like frost on the ground appeared on the desert floor.* (Ex.16:14 NIV) *He said to them, "This is what the LORD commanded: 'Tomorrow is to be a day of rest, a holy Sabbath to the LORD. So <u>bake what you want to bake and boil what you want to boil.</u> Save whatever is left and keep it until morning."* (Ex.16:23 NIV) *The manna was like coriander seed and looked like resin. The people went around gathering it, and then ground it in a hand mill or crushed it in a mortar. They cooked it in a pot or made it into cakes. And it tasted like something made with olive oil.* (Num. 11:7-8 NIV) In contrast, the new bread that came down from God was not a natural substance, but rather a spiritual one that gave life to the hearers. Was this bread of heaven the natural body that Jesus walked around in? If you listen to Christian religious doctrine you would think so. Remember John Chapter One; "In the beginning was the word." Jesus was not a mere man as they saw him, but simply came as a man to fulfill the requirement of the last Passover. In his place in the Godhead he is not a man but the word of God. He is that person in The

"An Examination of John 6"

Trinity that speaks into existence the mind of God. If we look at Jesus as just a man, then we will continue to misunderstand who he really is. Jesus continues his discourse. *Then Jesus declared, "I am the bread of life. He who comes to me will never go hungry, and he who believes in me will never be thirsty. But as I told you, you have seen me and still you do not believe.* (John 6:35-36 NIV)

Here Jesus declares that he is the bread of life. Was he speaking figuratively or was he speaking about his body? Or was it something else about him that he was referring to?

Notice the statements of Jesus in the verses above. Will never go hungry and will never be thirsty, are statements he said right after he said "I am the bread of life." Was he referring to natural hunger and natural thirst? Was he promising that we would never go without food or water as long as we are Christians? I do not think that is the case and I have not read any Bible commentary stating it to be so. Then what did he mean? If I eat a communion wafer or cracker I will surely not be sated from my hunger, and if I drink of the cup, I will thirst again. If however, water is meant here, we have a different problem altogether because we have no ceremony or ritual for drinking the water of life. Why is it that with all the Scripture speaking of living water, water of life etc.; we have never made up a ritual or ceremony to represent it? In the Gospel of John 4:7 we read about the Samaritan women who met Jesus at the well. *When a Samaritan woman came to draw water, Jesus said to her, "Will you give me a drink?" Jesus answered her, "If you knew the gift of*

God and who it is that asks you for a drink, you would have asked him and he would have given you living water." Jesus answered, "Everyone who drinks this water will be thirsty again, but whoever drinks the water I give him will never thirst. Indeed, the water I give him will become in him a spring of water welling up to eternal life." (John 4:7, 10, 13-14 NIV) The question becomes what is this water and how do I get a drink? The answer is he was not speaking about natural water no more than he was speaking about his natural body when he said "this is my body." If his reference was to natural water, then we better do all we can to find that water, or make a ceremony or ritual in which by blessing the water we turn it into that water he was speaking of. Why? Because he said that the water would become a spring unto eternal life. How can we have eternal life without that water? How long will we be dull of hearing and insist on totally missing the meaning of Jesus words?

At this the Jews began to grumble about him because he said, "I am the bread that came down from heaven." (John 6:41 NIV)

The Jews didn't understand him anymore than most people understand him today. While we have ceased doing most of the works of the law, there are a few we insist on keeping in some form or another. Some instead of sacrificing animals, they indulge themselves in good works as their way of being forgiven and earning their place in the kingdom of God. But the Scripture plainly teaches that it is not by works. What is it about that teaching people don't understand? Why do they continue in things that will do them no good when they stand before God? There are those who still insist on observing days and seasons and years, that according to Paul we should cease to do. These were Sabbaths, feast days, Passovers, etc.

But now that you know God—or rather are known by God—how is it that you are turning back to those weak and miserable principles? Do you wish to be enslaved by them all over again? You are observing special days and months and seasons and years! I fear for you, that somehow I have wasted my efforts on you. (Gal. 4:9-11 NIV) Paul speaks very pointedly to these Galatians who have erred from the truth. By his words, he seems very disappointed and weary in spirit over them. My question is, what is it about man that he cannot accept being free? It seems he always wants to be in bondage to something, whether it is sin or a religion. *They said, "Is this not Jesus, the son of Joseph, whose father and mother we know? How can he now say, 'I came down from heaven'?" "Stop grumbling among yourselves," Jesus answered. "No one can come to me unless the Father who sent me draws him, and I will raise him up at the last day. It is written in the Prophets: 'They will all be taught by God.' Everyone who listens to the Father and learns from him comes to me. No one has seen the Father except the one who is from God; only he has seen the Father. I tell you the truth; he who believes has everlasting life. I am the bread of life. Your forefathers ate the manna in the desert, yet they died. But here is the bread that comes down from heaven, which a man may eat and not die. I am the living bread that came down from heaven. If anyone eats of this bread, he will live forever. This bread is my flesh, which I will give for the life of the world." (John 6:42-68* NIV)

Jesus tells them plainly that the bread that their fathers ate did not give them eternal life. They all died because it was not that bread from heaven. He tells them that the bread is his flesh, which he will give for the life of the world. We have to refer back to John Chapter One to find a definitive answer to this statement. In verse fourteen a statement is made that explains it fully. *<u>The Word became flesh</u> and made his dwelling among us. We have seen his glory, the glory of the One and Only, who came from the Father, full of grace and truth.* (John 1:14 NIV) The word became flesh is an astounding statement. The Greek used here for word is "logos". The meaning is a revelation in itself. According to Vines word studies, the meaning is full and rich. 1. logos denotes (I) "the expression of thought"—not the mere name of an object—(a) as embodying a conception or idea, e.g., and (2) the phrase "the word of the Lord," i.e., the revealed will of God (very frequent in the OT), is used of a direct revelation given by Christ.[8] (According to Vincent's Word Studies of the New Testament on John 1:14) Was made flesh (σὰρξ ἐγένετο) (Revised Version KJV)., "became flesh." The same verb as in Joh_1:3. All things became through Him; He in turn became flesh. "He became that which first became through Him." In becoming, he did not cease to be the Eternal Word. His divine nature was not laid aside. In becoming flesh he did not part with the rational soul of man. Retaining all the essential properties of the Word, he entered into a new mode of being, not a new being."[9]

The definitions given above speak of Jesus being the very revelation of God. His mission was to reveal the self existing one to us in a way we could understand as much as possible. The Word became flesh and made His dwelling among us. He came to reveal God to us through language. Communing with us, revealing himself to us that we might know him.

Then the Jews began to argue sharply among themselves, "How can this man give us his flesh to eat?" (John 6:52 NIV) This verse is particularly interesting when we understand why the Jews objected to his statement. It would have been against all their teaching to eat human flesh or to drink blood. They could not eat an unclean animal, let alone human flesh. They were also prohibited from eating blood, which had to be completely drained from the animals they ate. So we can see how this caused them to wonder at what he said. At least they understood that he must have meant something else, because they asked the question; "how can this man give us his flesh to eat?" (Jn. 6:52 NIV) *Jesus said to them, "I tell you the truth, unless you eat the flesh of the Son of Man and drink his blood; you have no life in you. Whoever eats my flesh and drinks my blood has eternal life, and I will raise him up at the last day. For my flesh is real food and my blood is real drink. Whoever eats my flesh and drinks my blood remains in me, and I in him. Just as the living Father sent me and I live because of the Father, so the one who feeds on me will live because of me. This is the bread that came down from heaven. Your forefathers ate manna and died, but he who feeds on this bread will live forever."* He said this while teaching *in the synagogue in Capernaum. On hearing it, many of his disciples said, "This is a hard teaching. Who can accept it?" Aware that his disciples were grumbling about this, Jesus said to them, "Does this offend you? What if you see the Son of Man ascend to where he was before! The Spirit gives life; the flesh counts for nothing. The words I have spoken to you are spirit and they are life .Yet there are some of you who do not believe." For Jesus had known from the beginning which of them did not believe and who would betray him. He went on to say, "This is why I told you that no one can come to me unless the Father has enabled him." From this time many of his disciples turned back and no longer followed him. "You do not want to leave too, do you?" Jesus asked the Twelve. Simon Peter answered him, "Lord, to whom shall we go? You have the words of eternal life."* (John 6:53-68 NIV)

The statement of Jesus in the sixty-third verse; *The Spirit gives life; the flesh counts for nothing. The words I have spoken to you are spirit and they are life* (John 6:63 NIV) is plain and to the point. The Spirit and the Words are what's important and the flesh counts for nothing. In other words, Jesus separated the flesh from the other two components. The Spirit and the Word would continue forever and give eternal life to those who received them, but the flesh was of the earth and would return to it. The flesh was simply a vehicle in which the Word and the Spirit was carried and was also that part that would be sacrificed on the cross. Adam Clarke commenting on John 6:63 puts it like this;

"It is the spirit that quickeneth–It is the spiritual sense only of my words that is to be attended to, and

"An Examination of John 6"

through which life is to be attained, such only as eat and drink what I have <u>mentioned,</u> in a spiritual sense, are to expect eternal life. The flesh profiteth nothing–If ye could even eat my flesh and drink my blood, this would not avail for your salvation. These words contain a caution that the hearers should not understand his words in the strict literal sense, as if his body were really Bread, and as if his flesh and blood were really to be eaten and drank. The words that I speak–Or, I have spoken. Instead of λαλω, I speak, I read λελαληκα, I have spoken, on the authority of BCDKLT, thirteen others; the Syriac, all the Arabic, all the Persic, Coptic, Ethiopic, Gothic, Slavonic, Vulgate, all the Itala; Origen, Eusebius, Athanasius, Basil, Cyril, Chrysostom, Tertullian, Ambrosias, Augustin, Gaudentius, and Vigilius Taps." (This is an important reading, and plainly shows that our Lord's words here do not refer to any new point of doctrine which he was then inculcating, but to what he had spoken concerning his being the living bread, and concerning the eating of his flesh, and drinking of his blood, in the preceding verses. Are spirit, and they are life–As my words are to be spiritually understood, so the life they promise is of a spiritual nature." See Bishop Pearce.)[10] His words were his flesh or the covenant and the blood was the seal that bound it for all eternity.

In summing up we can see concerning this subject; that it is not hard to understand the dilemma of those who heard Jesus' words at the last Passover and those who have pondered them for centuries since. The one ordinance that was necessary at Passover was that the lamb must be eaten and nothing could be left until morning. If there were not enough people in a family, as said previously, others were invited so that all would be eaten that night. According to Smiths Bible Dictionary[11] (The Passover was useless unless eaten, so we live upon the Lord Jesus Christ). This was the difficulty, how can we do this? I am convinced we don't do it with wafers or unleavened bread, or any other type of literal bread. Neither can we drink his blood by taking grape juice nor wine, whichever the case may be. The answer to the dilemma is found in understanding what should be eaten. Was Jesus talking about the bread he was holding in his hand and the wine he offered to them in the cup? I think not.

Chapter Seven

"TAKE, EAT, THIS IS MY BODY"

We will now examine the Scriptures used in the Communion service as well as those used to substantiate the doctrine itself. Before we do that, however, we must look at the doctrine of transubstantiation to have a full understanding of where it began. I spoke of this doctrine briefly in a previous chapter as to what it states concerning the elements of the sacrament. Here, I will concern myself with its origins. Innocent III was the Pope from 1160-1216 A.D. and under his reign; the Catholic Church reached the height of its authority. He inspired the Fourth Crusade, and against his wishes the crusaders conquered Constantinople and set up the Latin Empire. He also ordered the extinguishing of the so- called Albingensian heresy in France, with the result of later opening the way for the Inquisition. He also proclaimed the dogma of transubstantiation at The Fourth Lateran Council in 1215 A. D., which stated that the bread and the wine of the Lord's Supper was literally changed into the flesh and blood of Jesus after being blessed by a Priest and eaten and drunk by the penitent. This was not made a doctrine until 1215 A.D. (Cath. Ency. Online) My question is, if this is a true doctrine, why was it not taught and practiced in the early churches under the apostles? The answer is, it is not a true doctrine. In order to understand this fully, we must take into account how Jesus related to his disciples. For instance, why did he speak to them in parables? Why did he use symbolism in his teaching? It can be answered by the Scripture. In Matthew 13:10-14 NIV; we find this statement by Jesus. *The disciples came to him and asked, "Why do you speak to the people in parables?" He replied, "The knowledge of the secrets of the kingdom of heaven has been given to you, but not to them. Whoever has will be given more, and he will have an abundance. Whoever does not have, even what he has will be taken from him. This is why I speak to them in parables: "Though seeing, they do not see; though hearing, they do not hear or understand. In them is fulfilled the prophecy of Isaiah: "'You will be ever hearing but never understanding; you will be ever seeing but never perceiving."* The use of parables on the part of Jesus was deliberate, because he had not yet been sacrificed. Israel was for all intents and purposes, still under Mosaic Law. Therefore he spoke to them in types and shadows just as the Law itself was used in the same manner. For example, the sacrifices of the Law were shadows of the real and true sacrifice that was to come. What the sacrifices of the Law could not do, the sacrifice of Jesus did once and for all. In Romans 8:3 Apostle Paul speaks of this; *"For what the law was powerless to do in that it was weakened by the sinful nature, God did by sending his own Son in the likeness of sinful man to be a sin offering. And so he condemned sin in sinful man."* (NIV) In another place, when lepers came to Jesus and were healed by him, he told them to go show themselves to the priests for it was a requirement of the law to do so for anyone who was recovered of leprosy. (Luke 17:14 NIV) Why would he do this when he had come to fulfill the Law? The answer is, until he gave his life and was resurrected from the dead; the Law was still in effect. The next question is, why did he keep the Passover? The same answer applies; he was still under obligation to the Law of Moses.

Matthew, Mark and Luke are the only ones who give an account of the Passover that he ate with them. John alludes to the Passover, but gives no description of it as to how it was conducted. Instead, he gives us the true meaning in Chapters 1 and 6 of his Gospel; as I have already discussed in the previous chapter. Let us look at the Scriptures that give a description of this Passover. Matthew gives this account:

While they were eating, Jesus took bread, gave thanks and broke it, and gave it to his disciples, saying, "Take and eat; this is my body." Then he took the cup, gave thanks and offered it to them, saying, "Drink from it, all of you. This is my blood of the covenant, which is poured out for many for the forgiveness of sins. I tell you, I will not drink of this fruit of the vine from now on until that day when I drink it anew with you in my Father's kingdom." (Matt. 26:26 NIV) The question has to be asked; were these elements of bread and wine simply symbolic of other things? They had evidently eaten a meal together and Jesus had partaken with them. It is evident that he had eaten with them because he said; I will not drink of the fruit of the vine until I drink it new with you in the kingdom. He had eaten bread and drank wine during the meal. Was that bread and wine somehow different from what he offered them at the end of the meal, or was he using it symbolically? If indeed it was a symbol, then what was it meant to represent? As I said in the previous chapter, it was explained in Johns Gospel Chapter 6. Jesus expressly stated that it was his word, which was who he is, that would be forevermore sealed by his blood that he would shed on the cross. In other words, it was the New Covenant in his blood that would give life to all who received it. Jesus expressly said "the words that I speak unto you are spirit and they are life." (John 6:63 NIV) If the sacrifices of the Law could not obtain forgiveness of sins then why do we think that the ceremonies or rites of religion can do what they could not? The standard reply of most Protestants is "we do not do it to obtain forgiveness, but simply as a time to remember what the Lord Jesus did for us." Because he said do this in remembrance of me. The question becomes, do what in remembrance of him? Partake of his body and his blood. But how do we partake of his body and his blood? I say it is not by eating natural bread or by drinking wine or juice, but by eating the word of God. Jesus declared *"that man does not live on bread alone, but on every word that comes from the mouth of God.'* (Matt. 4:4 NIV) *Jesus said; I am the living bread that came down from heaven. If anyone eats of this bread, he will live forever. This bread is my flesh, which I will give for the life of the world.* (John 6:51 NIV) The question that was asked is how are we to do this? Can we eat his flesh and drink his blood? What a dilemma was created for those who heard him speak that day. They could not understand him and began to question among themselves what this meant. We are still asking the same question today. Pope Innocent III thought he found the answer when the doctrine of transubstantiation was introduced in 1215 A.D. Evidently, the question was at the forefront of religious thought for twelve centuries after Christ. If it wasn't, why did they come up with what they thought was the answer? Their minds were just as dull as those who heard Jesus say it in person. They were still asking; how can we eat this man's flesh and drink his blood? Their answer was that we will bless the bread and the wine, and by a miraculous transformation, it will be turned into the real flesh and blood of Jesus. It really is the only answer that makes sense to the carnal mind if you take what Jesus said literally and do not understand it in a symbolical sense as he intended. The loaf of bread was a symbol of his word and the wine was a symbol of his blood. If Jesus had not spoken to us with words then we would never have known him. He was literally Gods word revealed to mankind, and the only way we can partake of him is by eating his word sealed with his blood that we might become the revealed sons of God.

There is another problem if we are to make a religious ritual out of what is termed the Lords Supper. That this was a Passover meal Jesus was sharing with his disciples there can be no doubt. That being the case, it was celebrated by the Jews once a year and is still that way to this very day. In the Catholic and Orthodox churches it is celebrated in almost every service. In most Protestant churches it is celebrated the first Sunday of each month. The question is, why is it not done once a year as the Passover was and is to this day? It is said to me all the time; "the Bible says as often as you do it." This is what is used to justify the frequency of the celebration of Communion. Paul said "as often", not do it often. It is also noteworthy that in none of the Gospels is the term "as often" used. The Gospel writers just said "do this in remembrance of me." We will discuss this further when we deal with Paul's full recounting of the Last Passover. As I said in an earlier chapter, the word "communion" does not denote eating and drinking, but talking. God communed with mankind through the intermediate agency of the Lord Jesus who by his own word declared himself to be the bread or word of God that came down from Heaven. So, as often as we partake of his word we have communion with him and remember him. It is sad that so many religious people only remember him when in a so-called Communion service. Most religious people can tell you the ritual of the so-called Communion service but have little knowledge or understanding of God's word. Jesus said; "everyone who believes in him may have eternal life." (John 3:15 NIV) Not everyone who partakes in a religious ritual. Jesus constantly stressed his word to those He was addressing. He constantly said; "if anyone has ears to hear, let him hear." (Mark 4:23 NIV)

"Take, Eat, This is My Body"

It was said of him "never a man spoke like this man." (John 7:46 NIV) It was never said of him; look how beautiful a ceremony he has conducted. He came with no pageantry, he was not dressed in royal robes and as the prophet Isaiah said; He had no beauty or majesty to attract us to him, nothing in his appearance that we should desire him. (Isaiah 53:2 NIV) He was greater than all that "He is the word of God that; became flesh and made his dwelling among us. (John 1:14 NIV) So when you think of what He said, "take, eat and drink from it all of you" (Matthew 26:26-27 NIV) get your word the Bible and began to commune with him or in prayer wait for him to speak to your spirit. Listen for his direction, for his comfort and his love.

Before turning our attention to Paul's discourse on this subject, I want to again bring your attention to John's Gospel on this event, found in John 13. For what I will be dealing with, we will concern ourselves with verse 2-9. *"The evening meal was being served, and the devil had already prompted Judas Iscariot, son of Simon, to betray Jesus. Jesus knew that the Father had put all things under his power, and that he had come from God and was returning to God; so he got up from the meal, took off his outer clothing, and wrapped a towel around his waist. After that, he poured water into a basin and began to wash his disciples' feet, drying them with the towel that was wrapped around him He came to Simon Peter, who said to him, "Lord, are you going to wash my feet?" Jesus replied, "You do not realize now what I am doing, but later you will understand." "No," said Peter, "you shall never wash my feet." Jesus answered, "Unless I wash you, you have no part with me." "Then, Lord," Simon Peter replied, "not just my feet but my hands and my head as well!"* (NIV)

John says nothing about the bread and wine but rather speaks of the washing of the disciple's feet by Jesus. This is a familiar story in Scripture and is often used to show the humility of our Lord. It is interesting to note that most of the major Christian religions have built no doctrine or ceremony based upon this passage. The only ones I know of that have are some Pentecostal groups and most of them have ceased to practice it. But people say to me, it was only an example and that is the way it is to be understood. Well, let's look a little further and see if that is the case. We read in John 13:13-16 this instruction; *"You call me 'Teacher' and 'Lord,' and rightly so, for that is what I am. Now that I, your Lord and Teacher, have washed your feet, you also should wash one another's feet. I have set you an example that you should do as I have done for you. I tell you the truth, no servant is greater than his master, nor is a messenger greater than the one who sent him."* (NIV) It is plain to me that Jesus gave them instruction to wash one another's feet. It was a direct instruction "Now that I, your Lord and Teacher, have washed your feet, you also should wash one another's feet". The question is why do we not have a formal ceremony for this in Christian churches today? The argument is always that it was a custom of the day to wash visitor's feet when they came to your house, as an act of hospitality. They wore sandals and walked almost everywhere they went, so this was considered a kindness and refreshment to guests. However, in this modern day we offer something to drink or to eat as an act of hospitality to our guests. Those arguments don't hold up here because it had nothing to do with hospitality. This had to do with a ceremonial washing before the Seder meal was eaten. It had all to do with the order in which the meal was conducted. In that day, they bathed before the meal. Adam Clarke says on the subject "He that is washed–That is, he who has been in the bath, as probably all the apostles had lately been, in order to prepare themselves the better for the paschal solemnity; for on that occasion, it was the custom of the Jews to bathe twice. Needeth not save to wash his feet–To cleanse them from any dirt or dust that might have adhered to them, in consequence of walking from the bath to the place of supper. The washing, therefore, of the feet of such persons was all that was necessary, previous to their sitting down to table; The Hindus walk home from bathing barefoot, and, on entering the house wash their feet again. To this custom our Lord evidently alludes."[12] The disciples had already bathed and Jesus was now washing their feet after they had walked to the place of the supper. If we are going to create a ceremony as to the eating of the bread and drinking of the wine then why do we not have a ceremony of washing the feet before the Communion which is a representation of the Passover meal? The meal is called Seder from a Hebrew root word meaning order. This is because there is a specific order in which the meal is eaten. The reason I bring this up is to show that what happened that night at the Seder. Jesus Seder with the disciples was much the same as what is done today. The meal is begun with

Kaddesh meaning sanctification. A blessing is said over wine honoring the holiday, the wine is drunk and the second cup of wine is poured. The second step is Urechatz which is washing. Today the hands are washed but in Jesus's day, he washed their feet. It was in this part of the meal that Jesus girded himself with a towel and began to wash their feet. The third part of the meal is Karpas or vegetable, in which a vegetable, usually parsley, is dipped in water and eaten. For the sake of space I am giving a shortened version of some of the explanations. The fourth part of the meal is Yachatz or the breaking. There are three matzahs on the table and one of them is broken. This is the part of the meal where Jesus took bread and broke it and at the end of this part the second cup of wine is drunk. This is the part of the meal I believe Jesus offered the bread and the wine. He used them symbolically, not meaning that we should get together often and eat bread and drink wine to remember him, but rather to understand the symbolism and partake of his flesh, or word, and understand that it is sealed forever more by his blood. It is a blood covenant that will never be broken. The only way we can partake of him is through his word sealed with his blood. If that is true, and I believe it is absolutely true, then why do we need a ceremony based on the works of the law?

Now let's turn our attention to what is commonly read or recited in the Communion service. It is found in I Corinthians 11 beginning at verse 17 and continuing through the end of the chapter. Many will say but it does not start at the seventeenth verse but rather the twenty third verse. Yes, admittedly the twenty third verse is where the reading always starts but that is because we don't want to deal with the rebuke of Paul to the Corinthian church about what they were doing and why Paul chose to address this issue at all. Reading from the seventeenth verse gives us the entire picture of what was being dealt with. I will here give the full reading for understanding.

1 Corinthians 11:17-34; *Now in giving the following instruction I do not praise you, because you come together not for the better but for the worse. For in the first place, when you come together as a church I hear there are divisions among you, and in part I believe it. For there must in fact be divisions among you, so that those of you who are approved may be evident. Now when you come together at the same place, you are not really eating the Lord's Supper. For when it is time to eat, everyone proceeds with his own supper. One is hungry and another becomes drunk. Do you not have houses so that you can eat and drink? Or are you trying to show contempt for the church of God by shaming those who have nothing? What should I say to you? Should I praise you? I will not praise you for this! For I received from the Lord what I also passed on to you, that the Lord Jesus on the night in which he was betrayed took bread, and after he had given thanks he broke it and said, "This is my body, which is for you. Do this in remembrance of me." In the same way, he also took the cup after supper, saying, "This cup is the new covenant in my blood. Do this, every time you drink it, in remembrance of me." For every time you eat this bread and drink the cup, you proclaim the Lord's death until he comes.*

For this reason, whoever eats the bread or drinks the cup of the Lord in an unworthy manner will be guilty of the body and blood of the Lord. A person should examine himself first, and in this way let him eat the bread and drink of the cup. For the one who eats and drinks without careful regard for the body eats and drinks judgment against himself. That is why many of you are weak and sick, and quite a few are dead. But if we examined ourselves, we would not be judged. But when we are judged by the Lord, we are disciplined so that we may not be condemned with the world. So then, my brothers and sisters, when you come together to eat, wait for one another. If anyone is hungry, let him eat at home, so that when you assemble it does not lead to judgment. I will give directions about other matters when I come. (NET)

In the first part of this discourse, Paul rebukes the church in Corinth for what they were doing and in order to understand this entire passage we must take into account a ritualistic ceremony that had become popular among the early Christians. They were called LOVE FEASTS and came more from the Jewish Christians than the Gentiles. These love feasts are what are being referred to in Jude. *These men are blemishes at your love feasts, eating with you without the slightest qualm—shepherds who feed only themselves. They are clouds without rain, blown along by the wind; autumn trees, without fruit and uprooted—twice dead.* (Jude 1:12 NIV) Adam Clarke, writing in the early eighteen hundreds, said in his commentary on this verse "The feasts of charity, the αγαπαι or love feasts, of which the apostle speaks, were in use in the primitive Church till the middle of the fourth century, when, by the council of Laodicea, they were prohibited to be held in the Churches; and, having been abused, fell into disuse. In later days they have been revived, in all the purity and simplicity of the primitive institution, among the Moravians or Unitas Fratrum, and the people called Methodists."[13] It had become a common practice in the early church to gather together for a meal and afterward; fellowship, instruction and worship. An example of this is found in the book of Acts; *On the first day of the week we came together to break bread. Paul spoke to the people and, because he intended to leave the next day, kept on talking until midnight.* (Acts 20:7 NIV) Breaking bread, or as we would say today, eating together, often took place before instruction in the Christian faith. This was no more than a common meal and had no religious significance at all. It was just a time of fellowship and usually occurred in the evening. What had begun to happen in the church at Corinth was not proper as they had gone beyond the lines of moral decency and Christian ethics. Some were gluttonous, others drunken, and others left out all together. Some commentators say that the co called communion was either before or after the common meal and had been corrupted by these ungodly actions. One who states this is Adam Clarke, who by the way, I like but do have some disagreements with on occasion, gives only one obscure reference to back up his contention. In his comments on Jude 1:12; *These men are blemishes at your love feasts, eating with you without the slightest qualm—shepherds who feed only themselves. They are clouds without rain, blown along by the wind; autumn trees, without fruit and uprooted—twice dead.";* he refers to a writer named Johann Kaspar Suicer (1620-1684) whose only work that is extant is a thesaurus published in 1682.[14] I admit I have not read this reference as it is only available in certain libraries, most of which are at seminary schools and can only be accessed at the school. The books are rare and have not been, as far as I can tell, translated into English. Clarke does not give the reading, only the reference so it is hard to ascertain any real meaning from his reference. Vincent, in his word studies gives only scriptural references as to the so called Eucharist and the ones he gives, in my opinion, do not speak to the subject at all.[15] One he gives is Acts 20:7; *On the first day of the week we came together to break bread. Paul spoke to the people and, because he intended to leave the next day, kept on talking until midnight.* (NIV) If you read before and after this reference it does not seem that this has anything to do with the so-called Communion service. He had sailed from Philippi after the feast of unleavened bread which was Passover, and had arrived at Troas. He stayed there seven days and on the first day of the week, which was to the Jews Sunday as their Sabbath was Saturday, Paul gathered together with the men of that place and broke bread or ate with them and after eating he spoke to them about the things of God. This had nothing to do with a ceremony we call the Lord's Supper. Another reference he gives is Act 2:42; *They devoted themselves to the apostles' teaching and to the fellowship, to the breaking of bread and to prayer.* (NIV) This refers to Peter's sermon on the day of Pentecost where about three thousand were converted to Christ and they simply stayed in Jerusalem fellowshipping, taking meals together and praying. His last reference is to Acts 27:33-36; *Just before dawn Paul urged them all to eat. "For the last fourteen days," he said, "you have been in constant suspense and have gone without food—you haven't eaten anything. Now I urge you to take some food. You need it to survive. Not one of you will lose a single hair from his head." After he said this, he took some bread and gave thanks to God in front of them all. Then he broke it and began to eat. They were all encouraged and ate some food themselves.* (NIV) He is trying to show that the early Christians often tried to blend a common meal into the Eucharist celebration but I think that is really stretching the meaning of these references. Too many times men interpret Scripture from their own bias rather than just letting the Scripture speak for itself. I really do not think Paul had the Eucharist on his mind when he fed the men with him on the ship. Personally, I can't understand his referring to this passage at all. I will say he said it was an obscure reference but I fail to see anything even obscurely referring to so-called Communion. I am always amazed at how far men will go to try to prove a doctrine they have very little basis for. How like the Pharisees keeping the traditions of men but not understanding the commandments of God. The facts of the story were that they were on a ship that had been in peril and had not eaten for fourteen days. Paul did not offer them a ceremony but gave them something to eat so they could receive strength. This encouraged them and they ate and were strengthened for the tasks ahead. So what was going on in the church at Corinth? An examination of the twentieth verse is needed here to illuminate us as to what Paul was actually saying to the assembly in Corinth. Here are the texts as they read from the NIV and KJV versions.

1Co 11:20 *When you come together, it is not the Lord's Supper you eat,* (NIV)

1Co 11:20 *When ye come together therefore into one place, this is not to eat the Lord's Supper.* (KJV)

This is interpreted by most to mean that they were just doing the Lords Supper wrong. They were having a full scale meal and not even doing that correctly. His supper is not a meal of natural food and neither is it when the food is reduced down to two elements of a meal, bread and wine. However, we must understand that the original meal which was Passover was a full meal and Jesus simply took two elements of the meal, the bread and the wine to show them a spiritual truth. The misunderstanding of Jesus intent has since gone on down through the centuries. It is evident Paul was not trying to correct the way the supper was being conducted but doing away with it altogether as evidenced by the twenty-second verse.

1Co 11:22 *Don't you have homes to eat and drink in? Or do you despise the church of God and humiliate those who have nothing? What shall I say to you? Shall I praise you for this? Certainly not!* (NIV)

He reiterates this in verse thirty four:

1Corinthians 11:34; *If anyone is hungry, he should eat at home, so that when you meet together it may not result in judgment. And when I come I will give further directions.* (NIV)

Paul stresses the point that if anyone is hungry for food, they should eat at home. He asks the question; don't you have houses to eat and drink in or do you hate the assembly of the saints? As I said previously, the argument that is put forth is that when they came together to eat is was just to be the bread and wine of the Lord's Supper to which I have already given my rebuttal.

1Corinthians 11:26 *For whenever you eat this bread and drink this cup, you proclaim the Lord's death until he comes.* (NIV)

This word "proclaim" means to announce publically. This is exactly what Jesus did at that last Passover. He announced his suffering and eminent death that would shortly take place. "The Greek does not mean to dramatically represent, but "ye publicly profess each of you, the Lord has died FOR ME" [Wahl]. This word, as "is" in Christ's institution (1Co.11:24, 1Co.11:25), implies not literal presence but a vivid realization, by faith, of Christ in the Lord's Supper, as a living person, not a mere abstract dogma, "bone of our bone, and flesh of our flesh." (Jamieson, Fausset and Brown 1871)[16] This supper was not meant to be a representation but an announcement of his sacrifice.

I want to turn now to the verses that support my contention and I believe are the key to understanding this passage. Notice that these verses are the very ones that are read in the Communion service and are used to support the ceremony that is conducted. 1Corinthians 11:27-31

For this reason, whoever eats the bread or drinks the cup of the Lord in an unworthy manner will be guilty of the body and blood of the Lord. A person should examine himself first, and in this way let him eat the bread and drink of the cup. For the one who eats and drinks without careful regard for the body eats and drinks judgment against himself. But if we examined ourselves, we would not be judged. (NET) Verse twenty-seven speaks to the eating and drinking the cup of the Lord by anyone in an unworthy manner will be guilty of the body and blood of the Lord. What was Paul's meaning here? It is clear that Paul is speaking to people who are professing Christ. But if we are truly born again Christians, how is it possible to eat and drink in an unworthy manner at the table of the Lord? Our unworthiness is not because we are sinners but rather because we cannot be trusted to keep his word. First, we need to take a close look at the word used here. It doesn't mean unworthy because of sin, but rather irreverence toward God's word. They were trying to make the love feasts practiced by the Jews into a seemingly Christian ceremony having to do with the last Passover. In Strong's Exhaustive Concordance we find he gives a reference to this. "(ἀναξίως, anaxiōs, an-ax-ee'-oce,

Adverb from G370; irreverently:–unworthily.)"[17] Webster's Dictionary gives this definition for the word irreverent.

(IRREV'ERENT, a.1.) Wanting in reverence and veneration; not entertaining or manifesting due regard to the Supreme Being.)[18] Thayer's Greek definitions says it this way; (ἀναξίως, anaxiōs Thayer Definition:1) in an unworthy manner;.[19] An unworthy manner is irreverence toward God and his word. Jesus had hardly ascended back to his father before the early Christians had begun to incorporate ceremonial worship into their gatherings. Understand that the greater percentage of early Christians were converted Jews. All they had ever known was the ancient ways of their fathers. Their Sabbaths Feast days, and Sacrifice etc. They soon forgot what Jesus himself had said to the Samaritan woman by the well. She said to him that their fathers worshiped God in this mountain and the Jews worship in the Temple in Jerusalem. Jesus answered her and said; "the day is coming when they will not worship in this mountain or in Jerusalem but the true worshipper shall worship me in spirit and in truth." (Para. John 4:23) This gives clear understanding of the Scripture concerning this;

He replied, "Isaiah was right when he prophesied about you hypocrites; as it is written: "'These people honor me with their lips, but their hearts are far from me.

They worship me in vain; their teachings are but rules taught by men.'

You have let go of the commands of God and are holding on to the traditions of men." And he said to them: "You have a fine way of setting aside the commands of God in order to observe your own traditions! (Mark 7:6-9 NIV) Our unworthiness is because we continue to allow ourselves to be controlled by the flesh and not by the mind of the spirit. Let me illustrate my meaning. We know that our physical body is controlled entirely by our mind. Every function whether conscious or subconscious; every movement, every action, all the internal organs are being controlled by the mind. If something goes wrong and a signal from the brain is impaired or a nerve is damaged and cannot get to the part of the body it is being sent to, we have a problem. I believe it is much the same in the body of Christ. All of our functions should be controlled by the head, even Christ. When the apostle said *"Let this mind be in you, which was also in Christ Jesus.* (Philippians 2:5 KJV) What did he mean? How can we have the mind of Christ? The mind contains the sum total of our knowledge which is simply what we have learned. Jesus' mission was to instruct men in the knowledge of God by teaching us how to know God and what his will is for mankind. To have the mind of Christ is to simply retain in our mind the word of God he taught us and do our best to obey it. The apostle Paul refers to this in his letter to the Romans when he wrote that they should not be conformed to this world, but rather be transformed by having their minds renewed. This isn't some mystical spiritual experience but a process of learning and understanding God's will for us. It's interesting what Jesus said about being yoked together with him. He said not only should we take his yoke but also that we should learn from him.

In the twenty-ninth verse, we find a pronouncement of judgment on those who do not discern, or as in the NET translation, without careful regard for the Lords body. It is not eternal damnation as some have supposed because of the way it is translated in the King James Version of the Bible. The word correctly translates according to Vincent in the following manner. "Damnation (κρῖμα) is a temporary judgment, and so is distinguished from κατάκριμα condemnation, from which this temporary judgment is intended to save the participant."[20] This is more of a correctional judgment that an eternal one. It is like a parent correcting a child that is being disobedient. Let me set up a scenario using what is stated here concerning the consequences of partaking of this supper unworthily. A non-Christian stranger or visitor comes into your congregation on first Sunday or as in some denominations every service, but they know nothing about what the service means. They are ignorant of the teachings concerning the Lord's Supper but because they want to fit in or not be embarrassed, they out of respect, partake of the supper with you. The question is, have they at that time eaten and drunk judgment on themselves not discerning the Lord's body? If, as in the Protestant world, we do not believe salvation comes through eating the Lord's Supper why do we believe judgment would come from eating it in an unworthy manner? Would God hold them accountable even in ignorance? Also, can we say that those who are sick, or weak, or who have died young in the congregation of the saints is because they have offended the Lord's Table? Paul says expressly, this is the reason that many of you are sick and weak and many have fallen asleep (meaning died). Try preaching that to a congregation. Do we really think that God would judge us in that harsh a manner for eating a wafer or cracker and drinking some wine or juice? If it is not really turned into the body and blood of Jesus as in the doctrine of Transubstantiation, which Protestant churches reject, then it's no more than a little flour and oil and the fruit of the vine. I contend that the ceremony this has been made into is not what Jesus intended. Let me give another scenario. Let's say there is a visitor in the congregation, or for that matter they could just be talking to a Christian who is sharing with them the word of the Lord concerning salvation. Or they could be someone who attends services and professes Christianity, but in name only. They do not really believe or live up to the teachings of Jesus although they hear the word every week. Whether they are hearing God's word for the first time or have heard it most of their life isn't the problem. The question is did they, upon hearing God's word, believe it, receive it and repent of their way and turn around to follow Jesus? When you are given the bread of life, which according to Jesus own words, he professed himself to be; you are automatically presented with a choice. You must now decide which master you are going to serve; the world and what it offers, or Jesus and the kingdom of God. My question is, how can you bring judgment on yourself by eating or drinking? However, you can do it by rejecting the word of the Lord. How anyone can read John 6, and not understand what he was talking about is a mystery to me. Jesus said it as plain as it could be said. While we carry on with our ceremonies the word is forgotten or paid very little attention to. We are like the Israelites that Isaiah spoke to in the first Chapter of his book. They were keeping all the ceremonies, but had forgotten the reasons for doing them. They were no longer paying any attention to God's word. People sit in congregations all their lives and partake in all the so-called sacraments of the church and still never come to know God. Why?

Because the sacraments are placed in importance above all else and the word of God is little spoken of or taught. I meet people all the time that can explain the sacraments but cannot quote a single verse of Scripture. Others can quote John 3:16 or a little of the Lord's Prayer. Some can even quote a little of the twenty-third Psalm but as to what effect it has had on their life is little evident. Many prominent ministers today who have large followings are no more than self-help teachers who do not speak of salvation or the kingdom of God. Their congregations are not taught in the word but rather how to become successful or have a right attitude, etc. While these things are helpful, and I am not against anyone becoming successful or working on making their life better, they are not the answer to finding Jesus as Savior and Lord. When we read or hear the word of God, we eat his body and drink his blood. His flesh is meat indeed and his blood is drink indeed. His word was his covenant to us sealed with his blood and a blood covenant will not be broken. To all that eat his blood covenant and believe in him will escape judgment, both now and in the kingdom of God.

Some argue they had just corrupted the "Lords Supper" into a full scale meal where some were glutinous some were drunk and still others had nothing to eat at all. They argue that Paul was just correcting them by saying what he knew about the last Passover Jesus had partaken in with the disciples. They were not to eat a meal but just take the elements of bread and wine together. If they were hungry, then they should have eaten their supper before coming together with the other Christians. The first problem with this is the Passover that Jesus ate with the disciples was a meal. The Seder meal is a full meal made up of certain elements that include more than bread and wine. That the Christians at Corinth had corrupted this into something it was not intended to be is evident but why did this happen? Because they were just like those who heard Jesus' words found in John Chapter 6. They said, "How can we eat this man's flesh and drink his blood? This is a saying too hard for us to understand, and many that day turned and followed him no more. We will always fail when we try to ceremonialize worship under the New Testament covenant.

I will now discuss what I believe Paul's meaning was, by looking at 1Corinthians 11:27-32. Paul states that before eating we should examine ourselves so as not to eat or drink unworthily. It is not recorded that Jesus said anything like this when he ate the Passover with his disciples. Jesus just said; take, eat, because at that point in time it did not matter because he had not yet been sacrificed or risen from the grave. The New Covenant was not yet established, for it was not until after his death and resurrection that it came into effect. Hebrews states this very fact. *For where there is a will, the death of the one who made it must be proven. For a will takes effect only at death, since it carries no force while the one who made it is alive. So even the first covenant was inaugurated with blood.* (Hebrews 9:16-18 NET) However, when Paul said these words, they did matter, for now men were held responsible for their choices, whether to follow Jesus teachings or not. It is beyond my logic and reasoning to think that eating a piece of bread or drinking a cup of wine would bring damnation to me. But it has been said to me, "it is just to be done in remembrance of the Lord, for Jesus said 'do this when you remember me". If that is the total truth of the matter then why did Paul add the statements as to judgment? Jesus simply said; believe in me and you will be saved but if you don't accept me then you will be separated from me." 1Corinthians 11:27 says that; if any man eat or drink in an unworthy manner, he will be guilty of the body and blood of the Lord." First, let us understand what an unworthy manner means. Does it mean that we are ceremonially unclean? Does it mean that we have sin in our life? My answer to these questions is emphatically, no. Then what is meant by an unworthy manner? Do we really believe this is the reason there is sickness and early death among God's people because they ate some bread or a wafer and drank a little juice or wine when not being worthy of it? The truth is that we could never be worthy of his body and blood. First of all his body and his blood are not bread and wine in the natural sense. The bread and wine were used symbolically of his body and blood just as Jesus used other symbols in his teachings. In John 6, as we have already explained, Jesus said he is the bread of life. He is the word that became flesh and had his dwelling among men. His blood was the seal of that covenant that bound it for all time to those who would receive it. It is the words that he spoke to us that are important. *The words that I speak unto you they are spirit and they are life.* (John 6:63 KJV) The way you eat and drink in an unworthy manner is simply this, when we hear or read the word of the Lord we are brought to a choice. This choice is not only necessary but demanded of us as to what we are going to do. We are either going to accept and believe his word or we are going to reject and ignore it. If we reject it we have made ourselves unworthy, because the simple truth is we are not now and never will be worthy, unless we accept Jesus and his word. That is the only way to salvation. The only way God can accept me is through the sacrifice of Jesus, and no other way. If I choose to reject his word, then there is left to me only judgment.

Finally I call your attention to 1Corinthians 5:7-8 and will give the reading in three different versions.

Purge out therefore the old leaven, that ye may be a new lump, as ye are unleavened. For even Christ our Passover is sacrificed for us: Therefore let us keep the feast, not with old leaven, neither with the leaven of malice and wickedness; but with the unleavened bread of sincerity and truth. (KJV)

Get rid of the old yeast that you may be a new batch without yeast—as you really are. For Christ, our Passover lamb, has been sacrificed. Therefore let us keep the Festival, not with the old yeast, the yeast of malice and wickedness, but with bread without yeast, the bread of sincerity and truth. (NIV)

Purge out the old leaven, that ye may be a new lump, even as ye are unleavened. For our Passover also hath been sacrificed, even Christ: wherefore let us keep the feast, not with old leaven, neither with the leaven of malice and wickedness, but with the unleavened bread of sincerity and truth. (RV)

In these verses, Paul is speaking metaphorically about the leaven or yeast as it is known today. He is not referring to the natural leaven or bread, but rather using it symbolically of things in the personality of men that should not remain if they have given their life to Jesus. He refers to the Passover as Christ who was sacrificed for us. Jesus is the Passover; he is the feast of unleavened bread, the word of God living in our heart and minds. It is this unleavened word the absolute truth that became flesh and made his abode among men, that they might be reunited to the Father God. The emphasis should be placed on Jesus, the word of God, and not on a ceremony made by men who didn't understand what was being said to them. Unless we eat his word sealed in his blood, we have no life in us and we will fall short of the mark Jesus has set before us. Jesus never said we would be judged because of a religious ceremony, but he did say this; *Therefore everyone who hears these words of mine and puts them into practice is like a wise man who built his house on the rock. The rain came down, the streams rose, and the winds blew and beat against that house; yet it did not fall, because it had its foundation on the rock. But everyone who hears these words of mine and does not put them into practice is like a foolish man who built his house on sand. The rain came down, the streams rose, and the winds blew and beat against that house, and it fell with a great crash.* (Matt. 7:24-27 NIV) He also said this; *Heaven and earth will pass away, but my words will never pass away.* (Matt. 24:35 NIV) Ceremonies will cease, religions will fail, but Gods word Jesus will endure forever because by its very nature it is eternal. Jesus did not say we would be judged temporarily or eternally by partaking of a ceremony unworthily, but according to Scripture by our words; *For by your words you will be acquitted, and by your words you will be condemned.* (Matt. 12:37 NIV)

Chapter Eight

**"The Spirit gives life; the flesh counts for
nothing. The words I have spoken
to you are spirit and they are life."
JOHN 6:63 (NIV)**

In the verse above, Jesus makes a very provocative statement. He said; "the flesh counts for nothing." In my opinion, this has been very misunderstood. I have read many commentators on the subject and their ideas range from; Jesus was speaking metaphorically, or to meaning the carnal fleshly views of men, and so on. I believe it was much simpler than that. Jesus was just trying to get them to take their attention away from his physical being. The Jews were looking for a king in the tradition of David, a warrior king to lead them to victory over the Roman Empire and to establish the kingdom of Israel again. They had even sought to take him and force him into doing so, but he would not allow it to be done. He is simply saying to them to pay more attention to his words for they are the true essence of who I Am, the Word that was made into flesh to dwell among us.

John, in his gospel spends more time on the subject of the "Upper Room" than the writers of the other three gospels. There are five chapters of his book devoted to the subject. However, John does not mention anything about the instructions concerning the Passover Supper. It was more than ten years after the other three evangelists wrote their gospels that John wrote his and even as early as this, people had begun to ascribe special or supernatural powers to the bread and wine. The only event common between the four Gospels is the betrayal by Judas Iscariot. John, as different from the others, does not speak of the Lords Supper. As said earlier, he gives no instruction as to any form or ceremony to be conducted. The other three evangelists give none of John's account in their Gospels. As I have said earlier, John spent more time telling us what Jesus actually said, and less on what he did than the other three evangelists. Only John tells us about Christ's discourse on his flesh being the bread of God that must be eaten by faith, for the salvation of man to eternal life. This is not the first time this was said in Scripture. The prophet Jeremiah wrote these words — *When your words came, I ate them; they were my joy and my heart's delight, for I bear your name, O LORD God Almighty.* (Jer. 15:16 NIV) The words "I ate them" come from the Hebrew word "אכל' âkal aw-kal'" A primitive root; to eat (literally or figuratively):–X at all, burn up, consume, devour (-er, up), dine, eat (-er, up), feed (with), food, X freely, X in ... wise (-deed, plenty), (lay) meat, X quite.[21] The meaning is emphatic and no other can be understood here. Other references are found in Ezekiel 3:1 and Revelation 10:9 as to eating the scroll and book containing the word of God. The only way we can "eat and drink" Jesus' flesh and blood is by eating his words by faith and thereby allowing him to indwell us through the agency of his Holy Spirit.

John also gives no account of Jesus' baptism as the other three gospel writers do. I think this is deliberate on his part because of the propensity of men to make ceremonies into idols. Just as the bread and wine have been misused and turned into idols, baptism is declared by some to be necessary to salvation.

Finally let us take a look at the word Jesus used in the sixth chapter of John. He used the word (sarx) rather than (soma) and the difference is noteworthy. In the discourse in John 6:53-58 Jesus uses the word (sarx) which is translated flesh and rightly so because that is what it means.

(sarx) Probably from the base of G4563; flesh (as stripped of the skin), that is, (strictly) the meat of an animal (as food)" [22], this cannot be understood to be the church, or body of Christ. He made it very plain by this metaphor what he was talking about was his flesh which in the first place had been the living word of God and had become flesh. (John Chapter One) This is the reason it was so offensive to the Jews who heard him that day. They said this is a hard saying and who can hear it. Even many of Jesus' followers turned from him that day and walked away. They simply didn't understand that he was speaking to them about his word; which if a man would eat, he would gain eternal life. It's interesting to note that Paul uses the word "soma" in 1 Corinthians 11:29 referring to the body of Christ. It is evident here in this passage by the context that Paul is speaking about the "ekklesia" (Greek for the called out ones) or the body of believers.

This shows there are two ways in which we must understand the Lord's body. First, we must recognize and eat his flesh, his word and be born again and then we must recognize who the other members of the body of Christ are, and receive and treat them accordingly. Paul said it very well in his letter to the Corinthian believers: *For just as the body is one and yet has many members, and all the members of the body — though many — are one body, so too is Christ. For in one Spirit we were all baptized into one body. Whether Jews or Greeks or slaves or free, we were all made to drink of the one Spirit. For in fact the body is not a single member, but many.* (1 Corinthians 12:12-14 NET)

I did not write this to condemn anyone, as I do not have that right in the first place. I simply tried to show a truth of God's word and to warn of the dangers of ceremonies and rituals that tend to, more often than not, take the place of what was actually intended. All you have to do is read Isaiah Chapter One to understand this is a real danger to true faith.

INDEX

Abel,
Abib,
abomination,
Abraham,
Adam,
animal sacrifice,
arrest,
artists,
beatitudes,
bible,
biblical,
birth,
blood,
bondage,
burnt offerings,
Cain,
Catholic,
ceremonial,
ceremonies,
Ceremonies,
ceremony,
child,
Christ,
Christian,
Christianity,
church,
clothes,
codicil,
communion,
covenant,
COVENANT,
creature,
David,
death,
destroyer,
disciples,
disfavor,
disobedience,
doctrine,
doctrines,
earth,
Eastern Orthodox,
education,
egos,

Egypt,
English,
Enoch,
eternal,
Eucharist,
Eve,
evil,
Exodus,
explorers,
faith,
FAITH,
false witness,
Father,
favor,
flesh,
flood,
garden,
generation,
Genesis,
genius,
grace,
Greek,
heaven,
Hebrew,
Hebrews,
historical,
Holy Communion,
holy of holies,
Holy Spirit,
hyssop,
idols,
immortal,

industry,
inheritance,
inventors,
Isaiah,
Israel,
Jehovah,
Jesus,
Jewish,
John,
judged,
koy-nohn-ee'-ah,
law,
law of Moses,
Law of Moses,
Luke,
Mark,
Matthew,
mediator,
membership,
Messiah,
mind,
minister,
ministers,
Moses,
Most Holy Place,
neighbor,
new moon,
New Testament,
Nisan,
Noah,
Old Testament,
ordinance,

organization,
orphans,
pagan,
parable,
paradosis,
Passover,
past,
Paul,
Peter,
Pharaoh,
Pharisees,
Philip,
Pilate,
priest,
priests,
problem,
promised,
protestant,
purse,
rain,
rebellion,
rebuke,
relationship,
religion,
religions,
    See religion,
repentance,
resurrection,
ritual,
ritualistic,
Rituals,
robbers,

Romans,
Sabbath,
sacramental.
    See sacraments
sacraments,
sacrifice,
sacrifices,
Sadducees,
Samaritans,
Sarah,
Saul,
scripture,
secular,
skill,
societies,
society,
soul.
spirit,
spiritual,
statue,
stimulation,
Strongs Concordance,
Symbolism,
system,
temple,
tradition,
Tradition,
tradition
trait,
transgression,
transubstantiation,
treatment,

tree of knowledge,
tribes,
truth,
unleavened bread,
veteran,
welfare,
widows,
wild beasts,
World War II,
worship,
worshipers,

BIBLIOGRAPHY

Adam Clarke's Commentary on the Bible. 1810-1826. Public Domain.

Strong, James H. Strong's Exhaustive Concordance: complete and unabridged. Grand Rapids: Baker Book House Co. 1987. (reprint)

Vincent's word studies. 1888. Public Domain.

Vine's complete expository Dictionary of New Testament words. *Thomas Nelson Inc*. 1996.

Webster's Dictionary of American English. 1828. Public Domain.

ENDNOTES

1. Strong's Exhaustive Concordance of the Bible Greek dictionary of the New Testament page 54 strong's #G3862

2. Webster's Dictionary of American English

3. Strong's Exhaustive Concordance of the Bible Greek dictionary of the New Testament page 42 strong's #G2842

4. Strong's Exhaustive Concordance of the Bible Hebrew and Chaldee dictionary page 110 strong's #H7523

5. W. E. Vine Expository Dictionary of Old Testament words

6. 1St. Samuel 18:7

7. John 18:10&11

8. W. E. Vine Expository Dictionary of New Testament words page 229

9. Vincent's Word Studies of the New Testament vol. II The Writings of John page 50

10. Adam Clarke "Clarks Commentary" Matthew to Revelation on John 6:63 page 564

Endnotes

11. Smith's Bible Dictionary page 486
12. Adam Clarke "Clarks Commentary" Matthew to Revelation page 617
13. Adam Clarke "Clarks Commentary" Matthew to Revelation page 953
14. Adam Clarke "Clarks Commentary" Matthew to Revelation page 954
15. Vincent's Word Studies of the New Testament vol. III The Epistles of Paul page 249 on 1st Corinthians 11:20
16. Jamieson, Fausset, Brown Commentary on the Whole Bible page 1213
17. Strong's Exhaustive Concordance of the Bible Greek dictionary of the New Testament strong's #G371 page 11
18. Webster's Dictionary of American English
19. Thayer Greek English Lexicon of the New Testament page 40
20. Vincent's Word Studies of the New Testament page 252
21. Strong's Exhaustive Concordance of the Bible Hebrew Chaldee dictionary strong's #H398 page 12
22. Strong's Exhaustive Concordance of the Bible Greek dictionary of the New Testament strong's #G4561 page 64
23. Strong's Exhaustive Concordance of the Bible Greek dictionary of the New Testament strong's #G4983 page 70

www.ingramcontent.com/pod-product-compliance
Ingram Content Group UK Ltd.
Pitfield, Milton Keynes, MK11 3LW, UK
UKHW041944230426
12048UKWH00008B/113

9 781626 979482